One Word Deep

Lectures and Readings

By Rebecca McClanahan

Delivered at Ashland University
Spring, 1993

The Ashland Poetry Press
Ashland University
Ashland, Ohio 44805

Poetry Books by Rebecca McClanahan:

Mrs. Houdini
Mother Tongue

I Dream So Wildly: An Anthology of Children's Poetry,
co-edited with Frye Galliard

Acknowledgements:
Portions of these lectures and readings have appeared in *The Arts Journal*; National Public Radio's "The Sound of Writing" series, 1991; *Life on the Line*, an anthology published by Negative Capability Press, 1992; and *Indiana Review*. Many of the poems included in the lectures were previously published in *Mrs. Houdini* or *Mother Tongue* by University Presses of Florida.

Copyright (c) 1993 The Ashland Poetry Press

All rights reserved. Except for brief quotation in critical reviews, this book, or parts thereof, must not be reproduced in any form without permission in writing from the publisher. For further information, contact The Ashland Poetry Press, Ashland University, Ashland, OH 44805.

Printed in the United States of America
ISBN 0-912592-34-6

For Audre Lorde (1934-1992)

While I was in the process of revising these lectures, I received news that Audre Lorde had lost her long war with cancer. Audre was my teacher, my mentor, and the strongest single influence in my development as a poet. At the time I first met Audre, I had already attended hundreds of seminars in creative writing, had published many poems, and had even earned a Ph.D., but Audre was the first teacher to ask me the simple, yet life-changing question: "How does the poem make you *feel*?"

She was also the first teacher to push me *beneath* the words. "You have language at your fingertips," she once told me. Then before I had a second to gloat, she spoke again. "What a shame," she said, shaking her head solemnly and running her hand across my manuscript. "The words are not here to serve you. You are here to serve the words. You must attend to the language." It was the most difficult and most important writing lesson of my life, one that I must relearn each time I sit down at my desk.

People are often puzzled at the powerful influence Audre had upon my life and work. "You are so different from each other," they say. "What could you possibly have in common?" I answer that *in spite of* our differences, we connected; *because of* our differences, I learned. Audre Lorde was Black. Lesbian. Feminist separatist. One-breasted warrior against cancer. I am none of these. Yet we do not have to be identical twins in order to respect one another. We need only be joined at some vital place--perhaps the head, but preferably the heart.

So, how does Audre's death make me *feel*? When I first heard the news, my reaction was disbelief. Although my head had long been preparing for the loss, my heart could not take it in. While my head was proclaiming, "She's dead," my heart was stuttering, "But no, she's too large, her spirit too difficult and beautiful, she cannot be dead, where does all that power go, where did she go?" I remembered a poem she had written twenty years before her death:

Hear my heart's voice as it darkens
pulling old rhythms out of the earth
that will receive this piece of me
and a piece of each one of you
when our part in history quickens again
and is over
>   --"Prologue," *From A Land Where Other People Live*

I've not yet had time to assimilate the loss, but I want to believe that pieces of Audre landed *here*--in this sentence, this book, in the poems and stories I have written, and in the ones that have written me. I dedicate these lectures and readings to her, with the hope that they may help dig the world one word deeper.

CONTENTS

One Small Grief   1

The Tale   19

The Word Made Flesh   23

Forever Yours   39

Jobs   43

Aunt   55

Composting   63

Hatching   79

What Is Not Ours   85

"The Earth is one word deep
                that is your name."
Alice Notley

ONE SMALL GRIEF: TRACKING THE PERSONAL RIDDLE

"Pursue, keep up with, circle round and round your life, as a dog does his master's chaise ... Know your own bone; gnaw at it, bury it, unearth it, and gnaw it still."
        Henry David Thoreau

In the beginning we are each granted one small grief. (Or think of it as our riddle, our bone, the heart's own work.) We tuck it into our secret pocket, rub it smooth, caress it for company when we fear the daily mundane world will cause us to forget. After a while our lives begin to sag from its weight, yet even if it were possible to toss it away, we would choose not to. Like the beast in Stephen Crane's poem who eats his own heart, we love it partly for its bitterness and partly because it is ours. And like the dog who hoards his bone, we trust that our grief will grow softer and sweeter if chewed to the marrow.

It does. Although we may grow into more profound griefs, more difficult, our first grief remains our first love, even if it is an unconscious grief, as mine was. An infant sister died the year before I was born, and I came into the world wrapped in her death. Twenty-five years later, when my first husband left me, my sister stirred in her grave. And when my grandmother died, the dust simply rearranged itself again. In "A Refusal to Mourn the Death, by Fire, of a Child in London," Dylan Thomas says, "After the first death, there is no other." So it is with grief. The first is the only; the rest are hand-me-downs. We may stitch them into a new pattern, alter them, shorten. But they remain the same old grief, quilted from the cloth of the first.

My grandmother, of all people, would have understood this. Every room in her life echoed the theory of redemption. She wasted nothing--not bread sacks, twine, old socks, egg cartons, tin cans, snips of yarn, rags from overalls, buttons and snaps. "Don't mess with my makings," she'd shout when she saw someone heading up the attic stairs.

Every year her nests grew. I'd tunnel into the cramped attic between stacks of bundled birthday cards and yellowed obituary columns, heading for the iron crib piled with her quilts: Star of David, Sunburst, Wedding Ring, Rocky Road to Kentucky, Crazy Jane. My favorite was a faded patchwork worn thin from many washings, yet fresh against my skin as if, when hung out to dry, it had trapped the sun itself within the threads. It had no preordained pattern, no fancy name. It was a simple quilt, stitched from bits of nothing.

Unlike my grandmother (and my mother and my three living sisters), I am not a seamstress. My poems and stories are my quilts; my art, the frame upon which my life is stretched. In *Moments of Being*, Virginia Woolf speaks of the pleasure that comes from discovering the unconscious patterns of one's life: "...a great delight to put the severed parts together...It is the rapture I get when in writing I seem to be discovering what belongs to what...the whole world is a work of art." It has taken me forty-two years to begin to trace, through the threads of my writing, the pattern of my life. Only now am I beginning to see how that first small grief has woven itself--indeed, continues to weave itself--through my life and art.

I first met my dead sister in a book, the way I had met Cinderella and Miss Muffet and Heidi. One day, shortly after I'd learned to read, I stood on the footstool and wrestled from a tall shelf the family Bible, a large heavy book my father read aloud from each Christmas Eve when he wasn't overseas. I had always liked its musty attic smell, the thin crisp pages, and the way the black letters fluttered before my eyes like birds. I turned to my favorite part, an elaborately decorated page marked with a satin ribbon. But this time the birds fluttered only for an instant, then began gathering in knots and clusters, lining up on invisible wires. The birds settled at the top of the page: "Births" was the word they formed, printed in what I recognized as my father's fastidious hand.

Her name stood out because it did not belong there. I recognized the other words on the page, for the names of my brothers and sisters were the first words I had learned, and my school note pad was filled with their names, printed painstakingly dozens of times in the thick black lead of my first grade pencil. A stranger finding the notebook might have assumed I'd been forced to write for punishment, the same words again and again. A stranger could not have known the delight that accompanied the task. My siblings were my world, their names the first litany, first poem I would ever write: Thomas Hayes, Jennifer Jo, Clarence Richard, Claudia Ruth.

So when I saw the strange name, Sylvia Sue, in the space after Tom's name and right before mine, I tried to brush it away. When the name was still there a few minutes later, I carried the Bible into the kitchen where my mother was slapping hamburger patties between her palms. I pointed to the name. "It was something in her heart," my mother said. "She was very small. She lived less than a week." Mother's answer must have satisfied the part of me that read books and printed names in school notebooks. I simply closed the big book and picked up where I'd left off, not knowing that the other part of me, the blind hungry animal part, would take a long time to be satisfied.

Several years ago, while spending a weekend at a mountain retreat, I was looking out of a wide clean window, admiring the expanse of green below. From where I sat, I could see the tops of swaying trees. I was eye level to the rustle and storm of thousands of tiny leaves, and for the first time I saw how hundreds of small trees, coupled with the invisible power of the wind, worked together to form this view. This is what I wrote in my journal:

"Some things we know only by their rustle. A small bird, a tiny animal moving through the woods, would be lost to us were it not for the larger movement which reverberates, swinging out like the many ripples in a stream made by a pebble. Trackers say that a small animal leaves little sign of its passing--a blade of grass turned down, a dry leaf flipped over, a broken twig. In order to be known, small things must announce their comings and goings, rustle something larger than themselves. When you drop your voice into an empty space--a cavern of mountain, a valley, a well--your voice answers back, made stronger because of the emptiness from which it springs. So we grow through the hollow places, throwing our voices out, to hear them come back again. We ripple and reverberate larger than we are. These are echoes we don't understand--to hear ourselves singing back as if from another self, some sister we have long ago lost, a part of ourselves roaming loose and free. The voice is akin to our own, yet it comes from a deeper place, and when it sings back, it tunes our song to a different key."

It surprised me to see "sister" appear in this entry, for I had not yet written any poems or stories related to this pivotal point in my life--the death of a sister. Looking back from the overlook of years, it seems impossible that I didn't recognize what I was trying to write--or, more precisely, what was trying to write me. The tracking of my personal riddle had barely begun. Yet the following poems show how I was working unconsciously toward this knowledge. As is so often the case, the poems were smarter than I. I am a slow learner; the poems patiently teach me. Here is a poem about a childhood doll, based partly in memory and partly in nightmare:

The Seed

Mother's belly that summer
was huge and creaseless
and the doll she gave me
was rubbery slick, its skin
stretched tight over stubborn
legs that would not bend and
sausage legs stiff in their casings.
I had seen missionary posters of
children swollen with hunger
and on our street a dead dog

engorged with August. Maybe
death was like a seed. Maybe
it was planted in Mother
and every night it would tick and tick
until finally it puffed her up
like the blowfish in the encyclopedia.
In the bedroom above, Mother slept,
the baby inside still faceless
as a party balloon growing
from someone's puckered lips
while I lay under covers with my doll,
stroking the eyes that would not close,
the swollen pellet toes.

Years later, I was present at the birth of my nephew. I felt all the emotions for which the Lamaze film had prepared me-- elation, relief, that Aha! moment of miracle. I had not expected to be ambushed by sadness, and certainly not by an event so maligned as the delivery of the afterbirth. But that is exactly what happened. As I watched my brother-in-law cut the umbilical cord and the nurses dispose of the placenta, a sadness overcame me. Later I wrote this poem:

Twin

Animals in their dumb wisdom
eat the placenta. Ancient Egyptians
worshipped it, preserved it at birth
to bury years later with the body, fearful
it would wander unmoored, forever
in search of its double. Doctors say
sometimes the placenta refuses to be born
and must be scraped away, dragging
with it the carpet of future children.
But usually it follows obediently
on our heels, this cake of blood
and memory, blind to the first light
we blink back. And when they cut it from us

and the seal of our mouth is broken,
maybe the cry that rises is a goodbye
to our dark sister who knew us when,
before the quickening, before heartbeat
or fingernail, when we swung
dreamily from the other end
of a veiny blue rope, joined once and only
with our twin. Wholly nothing, but whole.

    At the height of the conflict in Lebanon, I read a newspaper article about the children in Beirut and how their dreams had changed as a result of the fighting. Then one evening as I was taking my accustomed walk, I noticed chalk outlines that the neighborhood children had traced on the sidewalk. For weeks afterwards I was haunted by images of lost children. Here is the poem that emerged months later, as a result of that triggering event:

Evening Walk

The children in my neighborhood
leave themselves on sidewalks,
their silhouettes drawn in chalk
the way police mark victims
exactly as they fall. They could be
my childhood paper dolls,
the ones I cut so carefully,
turning the blunt scissors
each difficult curve, respecting
the slim necks
and what one slip would mean.

In Beirut children dream shells and cannons,
believing the butterflies are dead.
And I remember the slant-eyed girl aflame
who once ran naked through
the six o'clock news, her arms reaching.
This evening I step as if treading

some sacred ground, though I know
as my eyes trace the outlines,
these are the ones who got away.
This one, hearing her mother's call,
peeled herself free of the pavement.
And this one simply stood and walked,
Lazarus bursting the bonds of
his graveclothes and moving
toward his astonished sisters.

I smell the sweetness of autumn fires
from chimneys that promise evening
after evening of children asleep
in fathers' laps. In Auschwitz
chimneys burned with the flesh of the young,
the chosen ones, thin as lost promises,
too weak to lift a finger
as Hansel was asked to do.
I walk and darkness settles.
Light blossoms in windows.
Inside, the children soften and fatten.
Tonight they have somehow slipped
through the bars, past the finger pointing.
Do I shout thanksgiving? To whom
do I bow? What sacrifice bring?
I remember how the near-sighted witch
caged the boy, fed him to bulging.
And when the day came, Hansel,
grown fat on goose liver,
pressed a chicken bone through the bars
and stalled the terrible dinner.

Looking back, I see that the overwhelming emotion in the poem is guilt coupled with relief at having been the one spared--the typical survivor syndrome. For a child born directly after the death of a sibling, this emotion makes sense. Although the poem deals with universal themes, it's not difficult to see how my personal legacy provided the emotional underpinning for the work.

"Like the back of my hand," we answer when asked how well we know something. Yet how well do we really know each mole and freckle, each dent on the backs of our own hands? Are we too close--and paradoxically, too distant--to see ourselves clearly? After my first book was published, fearing that I had been viewing through too close a lens, I decided to push away from the details of my life. Perhaps, I thought, I could discover harder truths if I stepped away from myself for a while. Apparently I had been feeling this need for some time, although I'd not been consciously aware of that need. Again, my poems were smarter than I, for within the pages of *Mother Tongue*, a book rooted in the voice and subject matter of self, lies at least one seed of dissatisfaction with the limitations of the autobiographical "I":

Trying to Escape Autobiography

"The truth is sticky."   --Nine-year-old girl

You would slide to a bluer place
or colorless. Write a cloud poem
mothers read rocking away evenings.
Boneless as cats dreaming or faceless
pictures a child connects
dot-to-dot in his mind.

But truth glues itself to the back
of your eyes. Just when you thought
you wiped the table clean, your elbow
catches in a smear of it.

This is the clasp and leech of real.
Mucilage. The daily molasses.
And who has dipped my wings in syrup
while I slept? asked the moth, breathless.

You want those made-up people.
But they limp your cousin's limp.
Every scent your mother's. Each breath
your father's last wheeze.
Bones clank through your poems,
their marrow sticky, dripping.

    My movement towards new poetic voices and forms was in several directions, moving backward thematically through mythology and history (as in the Biblical Leah, Mrs. Houdini, and the seven wives of Zeus), while at the same time moving forward into contemporary voices (a clay eater, a present-day mistress, and a modern Japanese woman). I had also begun experimenting with traditional forms--couplets, sestinas, envelope quatrains, and more. Paradoxically, while working in these stricter forms, especially in writing the persona poems, I found a freedom to say much of what I had been unable to say in my first book. And what a profound relief to speak through other women's voices! In most cases the women in the poems were brighter, bolder, more beautiful and strong than I--and infinitely wiser.
    Still, no matter how hard I tried to get away from my one small grief, I could not. The work kept pulling me back--even when the informants were not women *per se*, but clouds or fish, or even, as in these lines from "Produce Aisle," vegetables in a grocery store:

In the center aisle, bananas in bunches
curl like firm young girls in sleep. Soon they will turn
like their half-price sisters, learn the bruise,
dark print that begins beneath the skin and grows.

Years later, each time I reread the poems, the women gather around me. Voice after voice they sing their stories, and the losses pile up.
    Mrs. Houdini waits by the fire for the spirit of the dead to speak.
    An aging farm woman stands at a stove making plum

preserves (the "skins slipping off in her hands") while remembering her daughters, now dead.

Leah mourns the loss of her sister Rachel's love after Jacob comes between them--("Jacob, the twin,/ who swam the womb in second place,/ clutching the heel of his brother")--a loss that engendered the nation of Israel, "a country/torn from the loins of two sisters."

A Japanese woman, in the tradition of *oya-ko-shinju*, steps into the sea with her children, but not before she speaks: "Together, our footprints/deeper than my own."

So it was that the women in my poems (and later my stories) walked with me, deepening the tracks of my personal journey. Our stories, it seemed, were the same story; perhaps my small grief was more universal than I'd imagined. When this knowledge finally clicked, it freed me to rediscover old work and unearth abandoned writings. An unsuccessful novel, completed three years before and buried in my study drawer, was resurrected in a new voice, at once personal and universal.

I felt as if I'd been speaking a foreign language for years and had suddenly discovered my mother tongue. And for the first time in my writing life, I began to care more about the work itself than about other people's responses to it. I took this as a sign that I was following the right trail.

The unraveling of my personal riddle would be incomplete were I not also to speak of the ways in which my work has allowed me to face childlessness. In my poems and stories, I shamelessly borrow nieces and nephews, renaming them daughter and son. The dead ones, too, I claim, in the same way that I once claimed my mother's dead child. After my sister Claudia's miscarriage, I borrowed her grief in order to write not only her story of loss, but mine, as recorded in a journal entry from that time:

"To bury an infant is to bury possibility, to mourn a life that was blown away like seed before it could be planted. You mourn not the child himself. What you mourn is what you must give up, what might have been. You must invent the life the child might have grown into, and for this reason, you will forever love this child. You bury with him no shame, no regret for things you did or said. He was in your life too short a time for mistakes; you never slapped him or sent him to bed without dessert or took away his bicycle. And, for his part, he remains as perfect as any child could be. He never stole your credit card or stayed out all night or screamed to your face that he hated you, that he wished you were not his mother. If a child must die, pray that he dies before his hair begins to curl, before with his first word (however clumsy or garbled) he names you Mother."

When the poem triggered by the miscarriage finally emerged, it was different in style from anything I'd written before. It is a chant, the simple rhythm of a child's jump rope rhyme:

Lament

How do I mourn
what barely was--

tadpole legs
swimming my sea,

pulse a muffled
watch's ticking.

How could I know,
how could I know

that years too late
this space would grow

deep below
my girlish breasts,

below my stomach
flat as this day,

flat as the name
stuck in my throat--

Rachel or Hannah
or Anna Kathleen,

my tiny seed,
my never girl.

My thirty-eighth year was a bleak one. I would find myself crying for no apparent reason, for hours at a stretch. Some mornings I could conjure no motive to get me out of bed. The printer's ink was still wet on my new book, but that just depressed me more. The poems in it were old. There were no new poems in me, and I was sure there would never be another. I also knew that there would never be a child. I could borrow nephews and nieces and students until I died, but I would never have a child of my own. When friends attempted to help me with my grief, I turned away or answered with a joke, bouncing puns off my nickname, things like "The Beck stops here."

One night during this time I had a disturbing dream:

I am a wooden Russian doll, stashed on a shelf. A little girl is reaching for me. Now she is twisting me in half, and I am breathless with pain. I try to call for help, but my mouth is only a painted mouth. The screams stay trapped inside my wooden head, reverberating louder and louder. Suddenly I feel a great release, the pain subsiding. I look down to see another doll emerging from inside me, a smaller version of myself, but with my mother's hair. Her mouth is painted too, and silent. Then from her middle, another doll emerges, then another, then another, until the last doll, the tiniest one, tumbles out, her mouth open wide and screaming.

Early the next morning I go to my desk for the first time in months. I feel weighted down, full to bursting. I pick up my pen and bear down on the paper, heavy with what my hand needs to write, and the words begin, pouring from my pen with an ease I have never known. Someone else's hand is writing them. I close my eyes and allow it.

When I open my eyes, names stretch the length of the page. They cling to the precipice of margins, swoop down upon themselves like buzzards. A litany of women's names. I rub my fingers along the page bristling with words my hand has written without my permission. Anna, Kathleen, Rachel, Lydia, Dawn, Esther, Mona, Sylvia Sue. The book of the living, the book of the dead. The lost lives and the redeemed. The ones given to me. The ones withheld.

That same year, for my birthday, my mother sent a necklace of myrrh beads from an Egyptian museum, along with a letter recalling the year she became pregnant with Sylvia, a year clouded with pain and resentment. The pregnancy had been difficult, the labor long and complicated. Finally, at the moment the baby left her body, my mother was sucked toward that tunnel of light which has since become a cliché to all but those who have passed through it. Whether it was the tunnel of her own death or that of her child's, she did not know. She only remembers the light pulling her toward it, and simultaneously, a resistance tugging her back to herself. Five days later Sylvia died. My mother was too weak and despondent to attend the burial. It had been snowing for days and the road to the cemetery was so rutted and snowbanked that cars could not get through. She stood at the farmhouse window and watched plow horses pulling a cart on which a small coffin bounced and slid. Life had closed its door in her face, and she was convinced the door would never open again.

But healing was taking place silently, invisibly, without my mother's knowledge. Six months later the cloud had nearly lifted, and when she discovered she was pregnant again, she greeted the news with joy. Life had granted her another chance.

My poem "Yes" grew directly from the information in that letter:

Myrrh is not a gift for the living,
so why these burial beads
my mother sends, thinking of me?
The night I was planted in her,
the dirt was fresh on my sister's grave.
Her name was Sylvia. I have seen the gravestone
nudging its head through the Illinois field
toward an immensity of sky. Sky
is all she recalls of that day, sky
and plow horses through the gray snow
and how No was the only word she could form:
No to her children and No to her husband
and No to her own next day. How it crept in,
she cannot remember, but next summer
she sat in church in a black crepe
maternity dress and said Yes to something
and light sneaked through her white gloves
and beneath her hat and she named me Rebecca,
from the Bible, a month before I was born

and August loped in, heavy and hot
as their Irish Setter with the one glass eye.
The day I was born she braided my living
sister's hair, walked my brother
to the outhouse and wiped him
and fed the chickens and milked the black cow.
She carried water in buckets
up steps from the spring house
to the stove, then down to the wringer washer
where dashers knocked, beating my father's
overalls clean. Two children at her knees
and one still rocking in her head,
and one in her belly pushing.

Through the process of drafting and revising the poem, several missing pieces began to come together in my mind, providing the first conscious clues to the riddle of my life and work:

Why as a child I was heavy with happiness, burdened with a gift I could not carry.

Why, in the middle of an innocent task--brushing my hair or feeding the dog--I would suddenly feel guilty, then guiltily relieved, as if I'd gotten away with something.

Why at night I talked to the dark, making up songs for the twelve dolls that lined the walls of my bedroom. Each had a name and a birthday I religiously observed and celebrated.

Why I woke hours later with a start, remembering I had forgotten to tuck one of the dolls in, forgotten to button a tiny nightgown or smooth a crease on a blanket, forgotten to tell one of the dolls goodnight. Or worse, spoken the wrong name or confused the birthdays of two dolls.

Why, when other teenagers would remember Jackie's bloodied pink suit or John-John saluting the flag-draped coffin or the explosion itself, the top of a president's head lifting off, I would remember this: the photograph of Lyndon Johnson on Air Force One, hunched over the Bible taking the oath, one hand lifted as if in surrender. The vacancy in his eyes as he is thrust suddenly into first place. The cloak of the presidency, the imperfect fit.

Then the long journey on which I labored to be bright and helpful, to love God and country, to win the prizes, to prove myself worthy of the slot intended for someone else, to earn what I am only beginning to see is unearnable, yet freely available--a love that began before I was born, while the walls of my mother's womb were still pulsing with the memory of Sylvia's body. And, only now, learning that the world is large enough to hold us both.

Salvage
   for a dead sister

I wore the bonnet knitted for you,
the hooded gown, your diapers
still folded on the dresser. *Congenital,*

the grown-ups said when I finally asked:
it was your heart that undid you.
Forty years ago, and still I haunt
the aisles of secondhand stores, past
bins of blouses, trousers torn and mended,
shelves of pointed pumps I squeeze
my feet into. Here, a stone dug in
too long. A run-down heel. And hobble
in some stranger's shoes home
where my husband--who came complete
with ex-wife and son--waits for me,
his face softening like a leather glove
worn just long enough. The world you left,
I use sparingly. Crumble soap slivers
into the washcloth, dig with a toothpick
the last smear of lipstick: small
resurrections, like the bedspread
I transform into a cloth for our table.
Now where someone's feet once rested,
there is this plate.

In the tracking of my one small grief, there has been no map to follow, merely the incidental signs left by its passing-- poems, journal entries, stories, memoirs. I offer them as a way of showing the power of personal myth to pulse through all that we write and all that we live. This is but one writer's journey, and it is far from complete. Already I feel the rustle of new works stirring. For instance, I've recently re-discovered the story of my Biblical namesake and am reminded that Rebecca was responsible for helping Jacob steal his brother's birthright. And yesterday the postman slipped through my mail slot yet another "Have You Seen Me?" flyer--but this time, there were two pictures. One was a photograph of a little girl who disappeared many years ago; the other was a sketch marked "Age Progression," showing the young woman she might be today, as imagined by forensic detectives using computers to extrapolate a probable face. What face might Sylvia have had? I wonder. Have I seen her look-alike on city streets, and is that why certain strangers seem familiar to me?

Other signs are beginning to reveal themselves, each one resonant with possibilities for future work:

The Nightstalker, a plane used in Vietnam and in modern-day rescue attempts. Painted black, it flies without lights and carries equipment able to detect the warmth of even the smallest body.

The image of the decoy lamb. Since an orphaned lamb has little chance of surviving on its own, shepherds often skin a dead lamb and place its carcass on the back of an orphaned lamb. The process is known as grafting and it literally creates a new coat for the lamb. The mother smells the scent of her dead lamb and takes the orphan for her own, providing milk for its survival.

Each of these images and ideas, taken alone, is but a small stone tossed into a large lake. Yet I trust that in time each will reverberate, spin circles larger than itself. Certainly I will grow into different patterns; I will not always write of Sylvia. Yet it is quite possible that her death and accompanying rebirth will remain the center of my art, for this one small grief with which I began my life holds within it enough fabric to last me the rest of my writing days.

WORKS CITED

Crane, Stephen, *The Collected Poems*, New York: Knopf, 1930.

McClanahan, Rebecca, "Evening Walk," *Mrs. Houdini*, Gainesville: University Presses of Florida, 1989.

------ "Lament," *Mother Tongue*, Gainesville: University Presses of Florida, 1987.

----- "Salvage," *Indiana Review*, Vol. 15, Number 1.

----- "Trying to Escape Autobiography," *Mother Tongue*.

----- "Yes," *Mrs. Houdini*.

Thomas, Dylan, *The Collected Poems*, New York: New Directions, 1939.

Woolf, Virginia, *Moments of Being*, San Diego: Harcourt Brace Jovanovich, 1985.

THE TALE

There were as many versions of the tale as there were tellers. Grandma's neighbor, Mrs. Sisson, made it autumn. She said she was walking back from the milking barn when she saw a black horse leaping a bale of rolled hay with my grandmother on his back, clinging to his mane. Uncle Leland remembered it as April, the last gray patches of snow melting by the mailbox. Great Aunt Bessie, Grandma's sister, recited it reverently as if it were a Bible story, focussing on the wound itself, the miracle of the quick healing.

But my grandfather told it best; on the subject of his wife, words sprang from him like a geyser. Although many women caught his eye over the years and one even held his gaze long enough to send my grandmother packing, Sylvie remained the only woman loved hard enough to inspire a tale. As my grandfather began the Mutt story, his brow smoothed out and his eyes turned browner. He gestured with squared-off, spotted hands. It was as if all his life had been mere rehearsal for this event, the telling of the tale. He pulled out all the stops, even when I was the only one listening, as I was that night thirty years ago on the wooden swing hung from the branches of the cherry tree.

Many years later, when he is ninety-one, my grandfather in his autobiography will trap the memory in black and white. By that time the story will have shrunken and toughened, pared down to bare facts: They had a dog named Mutt. He caught his leg on a fence. Someone saved him. My grandmother amputated his leg.

When I read this version, I will be flattened with disappointment. "It's Grandpa's age," I'll think, blaming the senility which was approaching at the time he wrote the book and which would one day claim his mind completely, except for snatches of old songs and poems he remembered from boyhood. I will use his senility as justification for my story, and I will hold strong to my version. Because I need it. And because, possibly, it is the real story.

"Your grandma got up early to fetch the eggs," my

grandfather begins. His voice is gruff, and as he sits down beside me, the swing bounces with his weight. A pail lies on the ground, filled with half-shelled peas floating in rainwater.

"She came back to the garage to feed Mutt, but he wasn't there. She called and called. Waited awhile. Then started to get worried. Mutt was always there. He might go wild all night, chasing 'coons, but he was always there in the morning. She waited some more, then went and got Blaze--no, it couldn't have been Blaze, must have been that black horse she favored. Well she rode all over the farm, way over to where the Sisson's land starts. Guess she knew something was wrong. She always can tell when something's wrong.

"She kept riding. Went down that steep path by the pond, and right when she was fixing to turn back, she saw him, all tangled in the barbed wire. He must have tried to leap the fence in the night. He was whimpering and yelping. She headed for the house fast as she could, there wasn't much time, he'd die by the time I got back from the sale, and the vet was hours away.

"So she galloped right up to the back door, even broke some corn stalks running over the garden like she did. She got the knife, jumped on the horse, and tore straight for the fence. Mutt was quiet, like he'd died already. She slid down the side of the horse, took that kitchen knife, held her breath, and just did it. Hardest thing she ever did, she said. Mutt was howling and jerking. She bandaged up the stump with her kerchief, got back on the horse, and carried him all the way to the house. She doctored him up and held him in the rocker until I got home. He cried all day. He'd sleep a little, then wake up and cry some more. But by the next day, he was sleeping real good."

Mutt lived many years. He died when I was seven or eight, but I still remember the shaggy black coat, the hopping dance as he ran across the field, the stump of his leg flapping behind him like a second tail. Over time, the house and attic continued to fill with my grandmother's makings--prize-winning quilts made from bits of nothing, hand-woven placemats and rugs, sock monkeys with their eyes stitched eternally open--but Mutt would remain for me my grandmother's finest handiwork. *The thing that you're sure will kill you doesn't have to. Cut it off. Stitch it up. Sleep awhile.*

THE WORD MADE FLESH

Lir, the God of creation, had only half a tongue; thus, according to Irish legend, the world began. I've always liked this story. If at least half of creation remains to be named, we writers have a job to do, some reason for being. This is a heady task. To be granted the power of naming is to borrow power from the gods, for in the process of naming, reality is born. Thus in the Genesis account of creation, the world springs to life through the voice, the word. And God *said* let there be. And there was.

But until the word "light" was spoken, the earth was formless and dark; "void" is the King James word. In this poem I explore the creation myth, proceeding from the premise that God was not only the first motherless child, but also the first homeless person, with literally no place to put his head, floating without boundaries in the cradle-less dark:

Order

Mornings like this I am grateful for margins,
for blue lines that separate. I know why
the asylum inmate, when handed a sheet of paper,
writes his name as close to the edge as possible.
God himself moved early toward margins.
Lost in galaxies of pure freedom, the first
motherless child called out to the terrible dark.
How good it must have felt when that first word
found its shape. Stopped. Cleared a space
for the next and next: *Let there be light!*
sweet baby talk of creation. And what a surprise
when chaos obeyed, split in two, the first neighborly
fence between night and day. Now there was something
to lie in, something to wake to, that first watery morning.
Day poured itself around him. His head was swimming,
where to put it? So Heaven was born, first hint of up.
Down followed soon, his feet sucked toward earth

where he rattled the first seeds into being,
divided the hairy clumps: Grasses. Trees. Herbs. Fruits.
Here was work to cut out for himself. Three more days
sorting the firmament into lesser and greater lights,
the waters into fish and fowl, into feather and fin, then
the endless multiplication of beasts and men which are yet
recombining. No wonder he named the seventh day
Rest! and gasped when he saw what he had done.

    Through naming, the world began; further acts of naming, finer divisions, generated the seemingly limitless worlds within worlds. In "Poetry is Not a Luxury," Audre Lorde speaks of the power of language to awaken the sleeping worlds within us. "It is through poetry that we give name to those ideas which are, until the poem, nameless and formless--about to be birthed, but already felt.... Poetry is the way we help give name to the nameless so it can be thought." Helen Keller, recalling her life before the discovery of language, questions whether wordless sensations can be called thoughts. She goes so far as to say that until she discovered that things had names, she was unable to love. Things were just things, people were just people; she felt no passionate connection to them. On the morning of her great discovery, Helen had thrown a doll against a hearth and felt a sense of satisfaction, even delight, when she felt the broken fragments at her feet. Later that day, as the well water gushed over Helen's hand and her teacher traced the letters "w-a-t-e-r," the mystery of language was revealed to her. "That living word awakened my soul... Everything had a name, and each name gave birth to a new thought... Every object which I touched seemed to quiver with life." After that transforming event, Helen's first act was to feel her way to the hearth and try to piece the broken doll back together.
    It is an ancient and universal belief that the act of naming is necessary in order to make something or someone *real*. To the Egyptians, there was no existence without a soul name, a "ren." Among the Netsilik Eskimos (to whom daughters were often considered expendable), once a female infant was named, it was

forbidden to kill her. And in an ancient Judaic custom, dead male infants (those who died before their eighth day) were not only circumcised at the grave, but also given a name to assure their share in the next world. The granting of a name, these traditions inform us, also imparts to the bearer a soul.

Last Memorial Day weekend, I was bicycling with my husband through a beautiful inner city cemetery not far from our townhouse. We often spend time there; the stone angels are mossy with age, the winding paths thick with oaks and elms that form an intricate latticework above our heads. Behind the groundskeeper's cottage is a section old enough to bear the headstones of slaves who once borrowed the names of their masters. In another section, World War I veterans are buried. Then there are the family plots--*family reunion* we call this section--where graves with shared surnames cluster, usually around a tall pinnacle engraved with the name of the oldest patriarch.

Until this day, we thought we'd explored every part of the cemetery. Then suddenly, as we emerged from behind a huge stone mausoleum, we came upon a sloped hill set close to the interstate and recently bulldozed, its raw red clay open to the sky. Pedaling closer, I noticed a row of stone lambs. We stopped, leaned our bikes against a tree, and walked over to investigate the graves. What we discovered was that they all belonged to infants, most of them dead within weeks of their births, some within days or hours. Each death was marked with a name except for one, the newest grave. In lieu of a headstone there was only a plastic blue flag (the kind landscapers plant alongside new grass) and a mylar balloon that had already begun to deflate. It was Memorial Day; I wanted to mark this nameless death in some way. When I returned home I scribbled a draft which, several months later, became this poem:

Infant Hill, Elmwood Cemetery

In the cartography of grown-up plots, six feet
the measure of a man, it is difficult to fit

a playpen fence, expensive to mow the uneven spaces
between. So on this hillside between public housing's
dusty porches and the interstate, the babies
are planted together. A truck rumbles past,
bequeathing to the asphalt slab the wrappings
of a tire outlasting its second chance.
On the fence, honeysuckle and wild roses
entangle in the perennial lust of summer
and a young girl walks the frontage road alone,
her hand resting on a white shirt shrouding
a belly which has swelled beyond expectation.
It is always a surprise, the seed that sprouts.
Always a surprise to bury an infant. What we mourn
is a heart that had barely stuttered, a blossoming
petal of lung, yet we must name him someone,
if only Infant Son of Sharon and Tim. This is enough.
Any more might sink the memory deep as these stones
promising too much: John Fitzgerald, Malcolm,
George Washington Carver the Fourth.
The newer graves are a comfort, soap opera's
brief bubble--Tiffany, Brittany, Jeremy, Hope,
names interchangeable as this row of identical
stone lambs grazing atop graves weedy
with forgetfulness. And here is a death too fresh
for a marker, except a profusion of blue carnations
beside a day old helium balloon with a few breaths left,
an exhausted valentine someone stood
in line at the grocery store to buy.

    Naming serves not only to impart life and "soul" to its bearer; it also grants power which must be carefully guarded. In some aboriginal tribes, children are given a secret name never uttered beyond their local totem group. If the name is spoken at all, it is whispered, lest an enemy overhear. For to know a person's name is to be privy to the secrets of his being and, thus, to have power over him. This is why Jacob, wrestling the angel, called out, "Tell me, I pray thee, thy name." Perhaps this is also why children invent secret languages and codes, so that they can own their secrets rather than relinquish them to the adults who otherwise rule their lives.

June Jordan calls poetry "your own naming of the world." To some, this may seem too powerful an assessment of the writer's role. Everything's already been done, they say. Yet even those who believe there's nothing new under the moon, no new worlds to be discovered, can find comfort in knowing they can give new names to that which has already been created. Children do this all the time, often without realizing it. One afternoon several years ago I had just completed a week-long poetry residency in an elementary school and was packing up to leave. The secretary came into the workroom and said there was a little girl in the office looking for the beautician. The secretary had explained to her who I was, but the little girl would not be satisfied. She *must* see me, *must* see the beautician. When I came into the office, I was surprised to see Lakeesha, a third grader who had been in one of my classes. I bent down and looked into her eyes.

"Lakeesha, do you know who I am?"

She nodded. "Dr. McClanahan."

"And what have we been doing all week?"

"Writing poems. I wrote four," she said proudly.

I waited for her to say something to explain the mix-up, but Lakeesha just kept smiling. Finally I broke the long silence. "Why did you ask for the beautician?"

She looked up, her brown eyes widening. "Doesn't a *musician* teach *music*?"

Then I knew. Lakeesha truly understood what we'd been doing all week. I had spoken of beauty, of the importance of seeing beauty in everyday things--the afternoon light ricocheting off your dog's fur, the sweat mustache above your brother's lip when he runs in from soccer. And Lakeesha had not only understood, but gone a step further. She had named her own world. *A beautician.* Of course.

Yet however apt Lakeesha's newly discovered phrase might have been, her insight would have remained uncommunicated if she'd not been able to explain it in terms I could understand.

The price we pay for communication is partial loss of personal expression; in order to be heard, we must employ a common language, one that stretches beyond our own idiosyncratic musings. Your dream last night, the one about the tap-dancing Anglican priest with the head of a tortoise who is speaking pig Latin, may seem fascinating to you; but tell it to your husband at breakfast and watch his eyes glaze over. Those speakers, or writers, whose only desire is to express themselves may just as well lock themselves in a closet and scream into the darkness. When you do not also strive to communicate, you are, as Frank Stanford puts it, "dancing with an imaginary partner at a meaningless dance to which you have invited yourself and no one else."

What if, however, you are able not only to rename your world but also to communicate your vision to others? That possibility is fraught with beauty, but also with danger, for to name the world in your own terms, to invent a language of your own, is a political act, sometimes a subversive one. It is what the greatest poets do, but also what despots do, and unprincipled politicians and greedy explorers and exterminators of innocent men. The act of naming is not one to be taken lightly. That old sticks-and-stones adage is a lie; words *do* have the power to destroy as well as to create. The utterance of a name can just as easily kill as resurrect. Ask Salman Rushdie. Ask Lazarus.

The little green puppet on the stage is spinning straw into gold, a trick he has known forever. His grotesque head is thrown back and he is laughing, smug in the magical secrets of the universe and certain that he will live happily with his prize, the princess's firstborn child. But within a few minutes the princess wrests from Rumpelstiltskin his secret name--and with it, his power. In the last scene, the little man literally self-destructs in a grand popping explosion complete with colored streamers. The audience at the Smithsonian theatre applauds, and the puppeteer, my husband, takes his bow. Backstage after the show, I help him restore order--sweeping up the debris from the explosion, velcro-ing Rumpelstiltskin's severed selves together. But the goblin's magical powers are gone, at least until the next show. I place Rumpelstiltskin on his hook and the bead eyes stare back at me, defeated.

We step out of the darkened theatre into the gold of a perfect October. It's a greeting card day in the capital city--sunlight splashing through trees, across the green, off the hats of street musicians and jugglers. Our destination is the lawn beside the Washington Monument. We've been told that this may be the last public viewing of the entire AIDS quilt, and we do not want to miss it: fifteen acres of quilt panels on which are sewn the names of 27,000 people who have died of AIDS in the past decade. This seems a staggering number to me, yet in truth it's only a fraction of the actual number of dead.

When we reach the lawn, thousands of volunteers, dressed in white, are busy answering questions and directing viewers to particular panels; some pilgrims have come thousands of miles, searching the name of a loved one. Each quilt panel is three feet by six feet, approximately the size of a grave. Some are simple, stark, bearing only the first name of the deceased, or a childlike message: "We love you, Tommy." Others are elaborate designs featuring stuffed animals, license plates, and even in one case, a cellular telephone.

A special force of volunteers called "Handmaidens" scurry among the 24-foot sections, making repairs with thread and needle, restoring panels that have become frayed or split and making sure that the names have remained whole. Watching the Handmaidens, I am reminded of the ancient Chinese gravestones called spirit tablets--literally translated "soul silk." On each spirit tablet was engraved the dead man's "true" name (believed to contain his essence, a name that was known but never voiced during his lifetime). Great care was taken to assure that the engraved name was not effaced, for if it was, there would be no spirit in the grave. To erase a man's name was to steal his spirit, his very being. We step carefully between the sections. Above our heads, loudspeakers crackle with the names of the dead.

This recitation began yesterday morning and has continued

nonstop, even throughout the night. It will continue until all 27,000 names have been voiced, probably until late Sunday evening. As a child I memorized a psalm, and it comes to me now: "He telleth the number of the stars; he calleth them all by their names." Hearing the names read aloud is even more poignant than viewing the acres of quilts. The quilt records the collective cost, which is, of course, devastating--thousands of men and women losing their lives on a common battlefield. But hearing each name read singly, followed by the next, then the next, reminds me of the loneliness of death, its individual cost: "Thomas Grady, Alphonso Alvarez, John Dixon, John Early, Jessica Pharmer, Hector Rodriquez." One by one, like beads a Moslem caresses as he recites the ninety-nine names of God. Or the "necklace of names" in Hindu observances. "Wayne R. McClusky, Benny Ruiz, Perry O'Brien, Jim Compton, Katherine DuPree." Single beads on a common string, counted one by one by one by one.

And in this counting, for a moment at least, the dead are resurrected. Perhaps this explains the strange mingling of emotions I am feeling--sadness at the loss of so many lives, yet exhilaration at the power of remembrance. Swept along in the moment, I tip a pan-flute player five dollars, then spend my last fifteen on a T-shirt that reads *The Names Project: Keeping the Love Alive*. I want to remember this day. *Remember:* the old word breaks open for the first time, and I feel as if I might have invented it. Re-member. To put the broken pieces back, the broken members.

In English castle dungeons one of the harshest punishments, reserved for the worst offenders, was the oubliette, a small, damp pit below a grille in the floor where prisoners were placed and simply forgotten until they died. A few years ago while touring Warwick Castle, I was so struck by the cruelty of this torture that I began to dream of it. Even after I'd returned to the States, the nightmares continued. Oubliettes entered my sleep every night for weeks, and I could not fight my way out. Meanwhile, during my daylight hours, I was trying to comfort two friends. The first was mourning a recent hysterectomy, the second, an abortion she had had

nearly twenty years before. What especially haunted the
second friend was the fact that she had never named the dead
child, and that for twenty years, she had been able to forget
the incident. All these elements came together in a poem I
later named "Oubliette":

At the time what else could I do, you say. And No I don't
regret it. Then why, twenty years later, sitting on your bed
in the middle of the night in a stone cottage in England,

are we trying out names for babies? We have come here
to be girls again, thousands of miles from our husbands,
and you have woken me from your dream of black taxis racing

backwards down empty streets. On their wheels no hubcaps,
only hollow sockets where fetuses twirl like pinwheels
until one cab slows, spinning from its socket a baby

who lands face-up at your feet. Medieval doctors would have
named the dream *hysteria*, the vacant womb gone roaming.
I tell you maybe it's phantom pains like an amputee chasing

the absent limb or like those cows milked by machine
who begin to suck their own teats. All night you carry
the child that could have been. You are certain it was a boy.

In the morning, touring a castle dungeon, we begin our
descent down winding stairs, past the racks, pulley and stocks,
thumbscrews and spikes, to the lightless pit beneath the floor:

oubliette. The word means forgotten. Here the doomed lived
out their last days. Back home our dinner is brown bread
and melons. We light candles against an early dark.

You are at the sink, scooping pulp and seeds into yesterday's
newspaper, when you name him John. After the boy, you say,
from twenty years ago, the father who will never know.

In the act of naming the dead child, the woman also gave voice to those memories which had, until that moment, been lost to her. For this is another power of the word--to resurrect that which has been lost. In his poem "A German Requiem," James Fenton says, "It is not your memories which haunt you./It is not what you have written down./It is what you have forgotten." So Elie Wiesel speaks the Holocaust horror again and again, bearing witness to what his eyes have seen, in order not to be haunted by what he cannot re-member. In the same way, once the woman in the poem *named* her phantom pain, it no longer had power over her. That which is alive, in deed or memory, can no longer haunt us.

This would be a good place for an ending, except that nothing is ever that easy. Sometimes words are not enough. There are wounds that only silence will heal, silence and wordless time; indeed, some wounds may never heal. On good days, I tell my students, "Words are power. The more words you know, the more languages you speak, the closer you get to the *insides* of words, the more powerful you will be." Is this true? I want to believe it, but sometimes human pain calls out to me, wordless, louder than any poem.

The Angle of Shadow, The Angle of Light

The hall where they are kept is a broken
wing off the main building
and in the last desk a boy named Achilles
is back from a battle with the school psychologist
who put him in Time Out for pissing in a sink
and beating his head against a chalkboard until it bled.
I am the visiting poet and this is the class
of Special Students I have been warned against.
Last night I read an artist's notebook: *The angle of shadow
must be equal to the angle of light*, so this morning
in my poet's bag of kaleidoscopes and prisms
and peacock feathers, I packed a hard black

stone and the sun-bleached skull of a cow.

Achilles: his nametag is my cue. *A hero from a famous book*,
I say. *The greatest warrior of all*. But the boy
is shaking his head, he's heard this before and he's ready
with a sneer--*My name's from a cartoon*.
Later in the teachers' lounge I learn he has been dipped
in the river more than once. His mother is gone,
he has gonorrhea of the mouth from his father,
and now when he draws a self-portrait
he sketches in fangs and fur on the palms of his hands.
When I touch him he flinches, the teacher says.

The first Achilles had a caretaker, a Centaur
who fed him lion entrails and the marrowbones
of bears to give him courage, but what can I give
this boy? And what do I know of battles?
My hardest fight is trying to raise a ruckus
between pen and paper, limping backhand
into morning. If words were enough, I would
trace them on bread and give him a bite.
Or like the ancient mystic, outline them in sand
and we would lick up the ones that would save us.

I want to believe what the Greeks believed, that
in the beginning, in the chaos of unbroken dark,
a tiny seed slumbered
and when night coupled with death
she hatched an egg and named it light.
It is said that in the midst of battle the sun itself
blazed from Achilles' head and his shout was brighter
than trumpets. But finally nothing could save him.
Not the shield fashioned by Hephaestus, God of Fire,
the greaves and helmet forged in darkness
and laid at Achilles' feet. Not even his cry,
although it reached his mother, lost
in the caves of the sea and immortally helpless.

As writers we want to believe that words will answer the pain. "Knock knock!" we call to the universe, waiting for the other shoe to fall, the familiar "Who's there?" But sometimes the universe is silent. Language does not come to our rescue. Often when this happens, it is not so much that words fail us; we fail the words. "Attend to the language," a master teacher told me years ago, and it took me a long time to understand why this is such a difficult task. *Attend. Attendant*: the name for a servant. We must attend to the word; wait, literally, upon it. Like those fish who hold their eggs in their mouths, we must become mouth-breeders, learn to hold the words inside us until they are ready to hatch.

Stanley Kunitz says writing is hard because words get tired; they must be "bathed anew," he says, "in the pristine waters." This reminds me of the hundreds of baptisms I witnessed in the fundamentalist church of my youth. "Except you become as a little child," the minister warned, "you shall not enter the kingdom of God." So we were all dunked equally--the teenager, the mascara-lashed divorcée whose bouffant dissolved beneath the waters, the banker shorn of his three-piece suit. We died to the old self, were buried in the dark waters of death, then were born anew, like babies emerging from the waters of the womb.

Proust said that a painter must become stupid before the canvas. So tomorrow morning all over the world, we writers will sit at our desks and become stupid again, searching better words (or perhaps poorer words) for that which lies beneath the naming. Starting from scratch, scratching from start, we will labor to unearth the words from their hiding places. Sometimes the words will show their heads and the universe will sing out its kept secret. More often we will fail. And when we do, we must remind ourselves that even Lir, the god of creation, had only half a tongue; how can we expect to have more?

The Word

1. Daily Bread

With milk each morning,
I cried for my word,
mouth open to catch
the wafer Mother dropped
on my hungry tongue.
I watched her teeth, straight
and white as the words she gave.
Her lips closed, split apart,
her tongue flashed out
then suddenly in.
Light, she whispered,
tugging the switch up and down
until my eyes blinked in rhythm.
She taught me *water*, *saucer*, *yes*.
Shadow she would save.

Today I wake, hungry.
Say *grotto* to me, I beg.
You tease me with *seashell*,
starfish, crab. But I need *grotto*,
the grit on my teeth, the growl.
Last month it was *hollow*.
Everywhere I traced it.

2. In The Beginning

Here in this windswept cabin,
stripped of television and toys,
our daughters are making a language.
On their haunches they crouch together
as if beside some ancient fire.
They rub their hands
and the first words spark:
Booca (bread). *Itsa* (I).

Hot. Cold. Hungry.
Soon they shiver, reach for *you*.
Join hands, dance circles.
Now a new hunger starts
deep in their throats:
a simple word for *song*.

3. Love's Language

Not flowers. Not the simple
picture our young son draws,
a rose opening soft as a sigh
to the lily's insistent pistil.
When you come
it is more like going
and you clutch me to tether yourself
to earth, swinging out, out
to the blackness of *in*.

4. Grandmother, After the Stroke

There was nothing left to say
after she called the porch a cemetery.
Her signals bred hybrids.
Now slippers are catacombs
and Ruth is Marge.

5. Voice Lesson

Somewhere you lost it
and must find it again,
the voice you were born with.
When the wind starts,
your strings will vibrate.
Now we will begin.

On your back.
Pant like a puppy

until your whole cage
Expands. Contracts. Expands.
You are a newborn,
chin loose as butter.
We will begin again.

WORKS CITED

The Encyclopedia of Religion, Vol. 10, New York: Macmillan Publishing Co., 1987.

Fenton, James, "A German Requiem," *Contemporary British Poetry*, Ed. by Blake Morrison and Andrew Motion, Penguin Books, 1982.

Keller, Helen, *The Story of My Life*, Garden City, N.Y.: Doubleday & Co., 1954.

Kunitz, Stanley, "Dancing on the Edge of the Road," Interview with Bill Moyers, from PBS Series *Power of the Word*, New York: Public Affairs Television, Inc., and David Grubin Productions, Inc., 1989.

Lorde, Audre, "Poetry is Not a Luxury," *Chrysalis*: Vol. 1, No. 3.

McClanahan, Rebecca, "The Word," *Mrs. Houdini*.

Stanford, Frank, "With the Approach of the Oak the Axeman Quakes," *50 Contemporary Poets: The Creative Process*, Ed. by Alberta T. Turner, New York: Longman, 1977.

FOREVER YOURS

My first motto was the best, the one I did for Gotch's Taxidermy. "FOREVER YOURS" in big letters, then underneath in little letters--"The look of life, without the trouble." That's when I knew what I was supposed to do. Words. Ever since I was a little girl, I've been good with them.

My blessing, Aunt Mag says. God gives everyone a blessing and with it a burden, to carry on. Not that I believe in God like she does. But words! Sometimes they just stream through me. It starts as a quiver, a bump at the bottom of my stomach. Then everything gets blurry and the words just come. Sometimes they're so perfect, it feels like they're coming from somewhere else.

Like the one last summer for Lady June Bakery. It came to me while I was eating cornbread and beans. I jumped up right then and wrote it down. Aunt Mag just kept on eating. She's used to my fits of inspiration. I tell her Poe got them all the time, but his were more like seizures. I love Poe. A few weeks ago Miss Kitrick loaned me his complete works and I read all the poems twice. My favorite's "Annabel Lee." I thought of using "A KINGDOM BY THE SEA" for the fish camp billboard, but I decided it was too much like stealing. Besides, we're ninety-five miles from the beach.

It's been a long time since a motto just flowed through me, like the one for Lady June's Bakery--"WARMING HEARTS AND TUMMIES SINCE 1948." Makes my mouth water just to think of it. And their business has never been better. A good motto should hit people where they live, Dan Steele says. Dan's the man on T. V. who does those early morning learning shows. I used to watch his course on Advertising, but after awhile it seemed too much like tricks. What I do is not advertising. It's my blessing and my burden.

There aren't too many twelve-year-olds who make money doing something that comes so natural, Aunt Mag says. And she's got a point, though it's not as easy as she makes it out to be. But if I can keep it up, I'll have enough saved after high school to go live at the junior college. I want to learn all the beautiful words in history, especially the names. Then I want to travel around to all the towns like ours and name the streets. Our town doesn't have street names--just "A" Street, "B" Street, all the way through "K" in one direction, and numbers in the other. The school's on the corner of 4th and J, and we live at the end of 12th. So that's my dream, and I try to keep it in my head. In the meantime, I'm struggling. Last night I read "Annabel Lee" three times. Tomorrow's Monday, and I haven't a clue for a new motto.

The weekly sayings are the worst, but it's hard to turn down a job, so back in the fall when I was on a roll, I said yes to Payne's Dry Cleaners and the Exxon station. You've seen those kind of signs--the big boards where you slide in the plastic letters. But every Monday morning they need a new one and sometimes I can't get inspired. I feel all boxed in. Lloyd Batson who owns the Exxon, he goes to the Dove Christian Church and believes we are put on this earth to witness, so I always have to squeeze in something about Jesus before I get to say what I want. I stayed up half the night last Sunday trying to get one to come. I finally came up with one, but it's not my best. "JESUS IS LORD. WE PUMP. YOU RELAX." Mr. Batson's proud of the fact that he's the only station in town that still checks under the hood. It's a lost art, he says.

There's an old black man who works at the Exxon. They call him Comfo-see, and I could never figure that out until Aunt Mag told me the story. About fifty years ago a black lady in town had twin boys. One was healthy and strong with shiny black skin. The other one was tiny and he coughed a lot; his skin was yellowish and shriveled. Jaundice, the doctor said, and *that*, added to the cough, meant he wouldn't live long. So the lady named them Comfo-see and Comfo-stay. The big one was Comfo-stay, meaning he had come for to stay in this world. The little one was Comfo-see. He came for to see the world, but he wasn't staying. But somehow things got twisted around and Comfo-stay died before he was six. Comfo-see's still working at the Exxon and he's a grandfather twice already.

Miss Kitrick wants me to stop doing the weeklies. She says I need more rest. I'm her best student, but lately my grades have been slipping, especially in spelling, and she worries about me. But if the truth be known, I'm not a natural speller. I can't pull a spelling out of the blue, some word I've never heard before, but once I see a word and make the connection, if it's a good word, I remember it always. And once I know a word, I believe in spelling it the way it is in the dictionary. I've lost jobs because of that. Imelda at Charmette's Beauty Nook wanted me to spell beautiful with a "y" instead of an "i." She said it was for artistic reasons, that she wanted people to think, "Oh, yes, Charmette's. Full of Beauty," but I knew the real reason. She didn't have a whole set of letters. She got one of those bargain lots, the brittle ones that snap apart when you try to slide them into the notches. Once the dry cleaners got one of those batches, but consonants don't matter as much as vowels. You can turn an "m" and make it a "w." And a "q" can be a "g." But vowels are much more important, and I draw the line on ruining a word like beautiful.

I talked Miss Adams at the Wagon Wheel into changing the name of the motel when the old sign wears out. The wheel stopped turning years ago anyway, and the water never dripped right from the fountain. I figure a motel named Rip Van Winkle would be just right. Even if people weren't planning on stopping, they'd see that sign and start to yawn, imagining those clean white sheets turned back for them. I wish I didn't have to do the dry cleaner's sign for Monday. It slows me down just when all these ideas are simmering. "A" Street will be Annabel Lee, and "B" will be Bailiwick.

See, words are important. If the words are right, they *mean* something, not just money and better business, but something that people can carry around in their heads, like an old Christmas carol. Take *Whisper Knits, Inc.*. Just listen to that. *Whisper Knits.* Whoever named that was inspired. Every time we drive by the plant and see that sign, I hear a lady's voice in my ear, like an angel in a hush--*Whisper Knits*. I see sewing machines lined up, hundreds of them in rows across a clean white room, and at every sewing machine there's a grandmother with soft pink hair, like the wispy stuff Aunt Mag uses for the Christmas tree skirt. The grandmothers all have powdery cheeks and plump arms and they hum while they work. Last Christmas my brother Brick got me an aqua sweater, and every time I look at the label, *Whisper Knits*, it makes me feel new and soft all over, like when I was little and Mama held me on her lap. I remember the feel of her, and her voice. I'd slide my fingers between her slip and her dress, and when I shuttled my hands between the layers, the fabric would whisper back. Mama couldn't sing very well--she could never remember the words--but she could hum, and she'd fill in with la-da's and doo-dum's, just in the right places, except when she stopped to cough. Her voice was throaty and as deep as a man's, which was partly why she died, the doctor told Aunt Mag. Some people can smoke all their lives and never get sick, but Mama's cigarettes caught up with her fast. Her name was Vita; Vita means Life. I looked it up in Miss Kitrick's name book. Which just goes to show that naming doesn't always work. Being named Vita didn't keep her alive. And I tell Aunt Mag being named Regina doesn't make me feel like a queen, but she says, "You're still young. Wait and see."

JOBS

I composed my first poem in the bathtub while I was trying to soak the color out of my kneecaps. I was seven years old, and I'd recently discovered that my knees and elbows were slightly darker than the rest of my body. This worried me; I wanted to match all over. I'd been soaking every night for three weeks, and although I'd yet to notice any lightening, I was determined to wait it out until the gray patches faded. In the meantime, there wasn't much to do in the tub--I was too old for rubber duckies, and bubbles lasted only a few minutes. There was nothing to do but think, dream, and make things up. A poem about kneecaps started to fizz in my head, but I pushed it down. (Even at seven, I knew there were certain things poems were not supposed to be about, and kneecaps was one of them.) Instead, I composed a love poem to Kevin Bostwick, the boy who sat across the aisle in Miss Ranney's second grade class. Kevin was the first boy I'd ever noticed besides my brothers. I loved him because he had wavy red hair and already knew how to form perfect cursive letters, exactly like the ones on the alphabet strip above Miss Ranney's head. I especially admired his capital Q with its curly tail drooping lazily below the line. Sitting in the bathtub, I was certain I would love him forever, and I do, for Kevin was my first muse. I still remember the poem, which I set to music the next night. It was fortuitously titled "God bless Kevin" and it went like this:

God bless Kevin,
God bless Kevin,
God bless Kevin
Through the night.

God bless Kevin,
God bless Kevin,
God bless Kevin,
Wrong or right.

When the last line came to me, and not only came to me, but *rhymed*, I suddenly knew I would do something wonderful with my life. In that instant my small world turned over, and I saw what I was meant to do. I would be a writer. People would buy my songs and poems, and it wouldn't matter if my skin matched. Who had time to worry about kneecaps? There was work to be done.

Thirty-five years later, I wonder how I made it back home to the words that were my first love; there were so many bumpy detours along the way. I wrote myself happily through elementary school and junior high, but it didn't take long to see that although it would be fine to be a writer, it would be essential to have a *job*. After all, there would be college tuition to pay, groceries to buy, car payments to make.

After a few years of unsatisfying employment, I began to resent the path I'd been forced to take. Shouldn't I be sitting in a garret somewhere, watching sunlight creep line by line across my sonnets? It was no coincidence, I gravely decided, that *job* was spelled like *Job*. How many plagues, locusts and boils, years of famine and flood would I have to endure?

Now looking back, I see how each job, however menial, taught me something about writing that I could have learned no other way. William James once wrote that we learn how to swim in the winter and how to ice skate in the summer. Learning, like life, takes place while we're busy doing something else. So it is that each circuitous route led me back to the place I needed to be.

* * * * *

My first paying job was babysitting (one of the few opportunities open to pubescent females), and for three or four years, I spent almost every Friday night in the homes of strangers. I never lacked for work. Good babysitters were a rarity even then, and word spread quickly: McClanahan's daughter is dependable, the kids like her, she doesn't have boyfriends over, doesn't charge extra after midnight, doesn't eat much, and she cleans up the kitchen when she's through. For my part, it wasn't a bad set-up, especially the early part of the evening. I got paid fifty cents an hour to play with other kids. (I never thought of them as charges.) We fingerpainted, played Chutes and Ladders, and wove potholders on miniature looms. At seven o'clock I fed the children macaroni and cheese and ran their bath water, a task for which I was perhaps overqualified. When they were safely snapped into their pajamas, I read them one long story and sent them to bed. Throughout all those years of Friday nights, I never experienced any of the babysitting nightmares my friends had warned me about. The kids never had tantrums or stuck their fingers into light sockets or threw up on the carpet. Even the dogs were cooperative. Everything went smoothly until I turned out the Humpty Dumpty night light and made my way back to the living room couch, where the nightmares began.

Suddenly, the house awoke. Shadows rose on the blank wall, and a breeze blew in, but how? The windows were locked and shuttered. Then purrs and clinks, hisses and creaks from the walls, from beneath the floorboards. Even the attic was alive! Didn't you hear that fluttering, a whooshing of wings? The phone jangled, and when I answered in my polite babysitter's voice--"Pratt residence" or "Jacoby residence" or "Hammerstrom residence"--a male voice breathed back, "Sorry, I must have the wrong number." Before replacing the receiver on its cradle, I stared at it hard and long, a senseless gesture I'd copied from the victims in horror movies. Then I tiptoed to the lamps, switching them off one by one until the room was so dark I had to feel my way to the couch where I had hidden a flashlight in the cushions. I sat this way for hours, shuddering when the furnace blooped on or the icemaker clanked into a new cycle.

Finally, exhausted by fear and darkness, I settled into a stupor. My eyelids began to grow hot and itchy. Sleep lay just beyond me, but it was forbidden, for I was in charge here; my employers were not paying me fifty cents an hour to *sleep*. What if the baby woke in the dark, crying for his mother? What if a fire began in the furnace room? What if the maniac who dialed the wrong number slipped in through a window and murdered the twins in their sleep? (I had yet to kiss a boy, but suddenly I saw how a boyfriend, however pimply or gaunt or sweaty, might come in handy.) I had never been so lonely. This was a stranger's house; even in the dark I could tell. The Jacoby's house smelled of rye bread and mothballs, the Hammerstrom's of dog fur and dust. The Pratt's house had a comforting smell--something sweet ripening, perhaps apples, mixed with camphor misting from the vaporizer beside the youngest boy's bed. Yet comforting or not, this was unfamiliar territory. Even when I'd finally settled back onto the cushions and pulled the afghan around my shoulders, I was still not home free. For I was not *home*.

Yet somehow the minutes, then hours, passed. I talked myself out of the fear, shook the afghan from my shoulders, and marched triumphantly to the kitchen where I lit the burner beneath the tea kettle. The blue flame flickered, then spread, completing its perfect circle. I reached across the kitchen table and switched the swag lamp to its highest power. "Come and get me," I spoke aloud to the dark. "Go ahead, I dare you." I glanced at the clock; just one more hour. I could survive anything.

Now it occurs to me that my first job may have taught me more than all the writing seminars, workshops, and academic degrees I ever completed. What better training for a writer than this? To sit for hours in a strange place, terrified first of the silence, then of the unknown voices speaking in the dark; to work yourself into a stupor of fear, loneliness, and helplessness, then finally to shake it off, ignite the small blue flame, and challenge the darkness. Then that wonderful moment--familiar headlights in the driveway, another human being connecting, the long ride home through familiar streets you've never seen until now, altered as you are by what you've lived through. (And finally this, the coda I cannot resist: emptying your pockets to see that for all the struggle, you've been paid almost nothing--and knowing that next week you'll gladly do it all over again.)

While working my way through college, I held a series of odd jobs, some odder than others. I sang solos for christenings and funerals, gave piano lessons to neighbors' children, and served as companion/nurse to an elderly bedridden woman from midnight until dawn. I also drove a courier truck for a typesetting firm, an experience which taught me the value of speed and efficiency, of training my eyes on the road ahead and delivering the goods on time, no matter what. Later as a clerk typist churning out invoices, I learned how to sit in a desk for hours at a time and how to let my mind wander--valuable lessons for a future writer.

Directly after college I served a short stint as a military wife, which proved to be my least successful career. As early as the second week of the marriage I sensed I had made the biggest mistake of my life, but I was not about to admit it. I would work harder; I would cook better meals, steam his khakis with a cleaner pleat. In my off hours, however, I would find a job. I would not become another one of those wives in our beehive apartment complex--*military dependents*, they were called. I feared this fate more than anything. My college diploma, complete with honors and gold seal, was wrapped in its cellophane package, but where would I get a job doing English literature? No principal will hire a military wife, my new neighbor said. You'll be lucky to get a job cleaning houses.

But my determination clicked in again, and within a week I had not one job, but two: telephone solicitor for Sears Catalogue Store and part-time Avon lady. My combined paychecks did not amount to much, but I earned enough to cover the initial Avon Representative Package (ninety-five dollars, which included the turquoise brocade satchel filled with samples) and to buy an occasional T-bone and bottle of wine for the Better Homes and Gardens dinners I plotted and executed each Saturday night. The flurry of activity, rushing between jobs, kept my loneliness at bay and left me little time to worry about becoming one of the wives I saw in the laundromat.

Avon delivered more than I'd bargained for. As it turned

out, my assigned territory was the army base; my clients, the military dependents I was so desperately trying to avoid. Once I rang the first bell and the chain was unbolted, once I entered the first khaki-colored apartment with the olive drab carpet and floorplan identical to my own, I could no longer ignore the lives behind the doors. Some women were still in their housecoats at two o'clock. Their babies always had the flu, runny noses, and impetigo; the padded slippers of their vitamin-stained sleepers had been lopped off to allow for three months' more wear, but the snaps were straining. The faded children clung to their mothers or sat mesmerized by the black and white static on the television, the antennae wrapped in aluminum foil in a desperate attempt at better reception.

And the more doors I opened, the more I found myself. The world outside my apartment, I discovered, was filled with people so eager for human company that they would open their door to a stranger, women so hungry for beauty that they would spend their grocery money on bubble bath and wait months for the back-order to be shipped. Here were lives waiting to be written, and my life was one of them. But I was not yet equipped for the task.

Instead, I sat at the formica dinettes, fanning colored brochures and pointing to monthly specials circled in red. If a woman said yes and signed the order, I felt worse than when she refused me. Not only would the lipstick, the nail polish and blush, the bubbling bath oil *not* solve her problems, but when her husband saw the bill, there might be more to pay. One woman paid her husband regularly; I saw the purple bruises on the backs of her thighs as she walked to the counter to pour more coffee. She was from Mexico and she spoke no English. Each time I visited she was wearing a different pair of baby doll pajamas and, thanks to me, a new shade of nail polish. Whenever I handed her a catalogue, her eyes lit up and while she waited for me to pull her order from the satchel she rubbed her hands together like a greedy cartoon fly. One day, in the middle of reciting the Christmas specials, I looked up to see her staring at me. Her eyes were lined with Midnight Blue, teary with admiration I could not bear. I handed her the satchel filled with six months of samples. "Feliz Navidad," I said. Then I drove to the area office and paid the balance on my unpaid orders. Thus ended my Avon career.

At the Sears Catalogue Store I spent my days dialing the homes of strangers, trying to sell them things they didn't yet know they needed. This was the last job I would have ever chosen. I hated phone solicitors; I'd always hung up on them. But now that I was on the other end of the phone wires, I convinced myself this was a worthy occupation and I began to map out my strategy. When the customers answered, I would cheerfully announce myself as their personal shopper, then set about to enumerate the current specials: thigh-hi stockings, bed ruffles, a thirty pound box of laundry detergent, cafe curtains, a ten-pack of men's cotton briefs.

It took me only a few minutes to be impaled on the wheel of my own karma. God was getting me back for all those times I'd hung up.

"Hello, I'm Becky, your Sears personal shopper."

Click.

"Good morning, I'm Becky, your personal shopper from Sears."

Click.

"Hello, I'm Becky."

"Becky? Becky Sanderson? Do you have a cold or something?"

"No. Becky from Sears. I'm your personal shopper."

"*I've* got a personal *shopper* ?" The awe in her voice! The promise! As if I'd announced I was her personal *savior*. Hurry, get it all in, the speech you've been rehearsing, before she hangs up. "Yes, I'm here to serve you. Allow me to tell you about the monthly specials. There's our Slim Boy's Toughskin Jeans and ...."

Click.

The second day during coffee break I cried into my cup and at lunch I locked myself in the dusty storeroom where I started in again. After a few minutes, I heard the jangling of a very impressive ring of keys. The door opened and Thelma stepped in. Thelma was the assistant manager, an energetic sixtyish woman whose pocketbook always matched her shoes. Sears was her life. She whipped a blue tissue from her pocket and offered it to me. "It's not *you* they're hanging up on. They don't know you from Eve. You'll get used to it. One of these days someone's going to need something, just wait. You'll hit them at just the right moment, they'll order the Queen-Size Double Sleep Set and the monogrammed towels and the four-slice toaster, just like that." She snapped her fingers. "In the twinkling of an eye. Like pulling teeth."

Despite Thelma's mixed metaphor, it was perhaps the best advice regarding the publishing world that I'd ever receive. I pass it on to you, free of charge: *The editors aren't hanging up on you. They don't know you from Eve. It's not that they don't want your poem or story. They just don't need it yet, or they don't know they need it. Maybe they're just having a bad day.* Put that advice in the satchel of your memory and pull it out when you need it, the way I did last year, and last month. And yesterday.

After three weeks on the phone desk, my strategy and luck had improved. One fine day I sold an infant's car seat and a power drill, seven packages of crew socks, and a plastic mattress cover. More important, on those days when I didn't sell anything, I still went home dry-eyed. I'd learned to separate my soul from what I was selling. However, the loneliness was getting to me, and my right ear was sore. I was tired of disembodied voices; like the military dependents behind the Avon doors, I was craving human contact, at any price. One morning during coffee break, I volunteered for the return desk.

"Returns? Are you crazy?" Thelma said. "Nobody wants the return desk. Are you sure?"

I nodded.

"You'll be on your feet all day. All you'll hear is complaints."

As it turned out, Thelma was wrong. Most of the returns

had nothing to do with the quality of the goods, and I rarely met a disgruntled customer. Some of the customers, in fact, had developed an affection for their merchandise and truly hated having to give it up. Their apologies were profuse and heartfelt, and I sympathized with their plights. I, too, was sorry that the draperies were too blue for the sofa, sorry that the bald man's wife had always worn a size eight before the baby. These things can't be helped. No harm done, I'd say, placing the item on the black conveyor belt with the same reverence I now use to pluck a beautiful but ill-fitting line from a poem or release a muscular chapter from its bondage in a too tight novel. The returned merchandise grew around me, the mere bulk of it cushioning my days. I'd check the "Reason for Return" box while I consoled the customer with the promise of new life awaiting the discarded item. "It will go back to the warehouse, then be checked and repackaged. Someone will be able to use it. Don't worry. It will find a home."

Sadly, however, there was some merchandise that never made it back to the shelves. The fact that this is a difficult concept for me to embrace is due in part to genetic inheritance. Since both my grandmothers were quilters and since my mother was the kind of frugal gourmet who emptied the entire refrigerator (every limp carrot and thimbleful of broth) into a stew pot each Friday night, I want to believe that everything will find a home. Thus, I've tried squeezing short stories into the girdle of a haiku; I've tried resurrecting lines that should never have been born in the first place, while this hard truth remains: Some merchandise--yes, even *Sears* merchandise--is clearly and simply *defective*, and there is no way to stitch it, hammer it, or glue it back into shape. Piled on my return desk were pantsuits with three legs, badly-stitched comforters, sunburst clocks with hands that ran backwards, and a blender that growled when it should have whirred. It was with sadness that I loaded these items onto the conveyor belt and watched each one disappear behind the huge black flap from which there was no return.

But there are new lives, always, waiting to be written. The last job I held before entering fulltime the world of writing and teaching was as organist for a military wedding chapel. Several times a week (more often near holidays when soldiers took extended leave) I lifted the heavy wooden cover, coaxed the sheet music into place, and serenaded one couple, then the next, into their uncertain marital futures. Of course the soldiers and brides did not see their futures as uncertain; no one standing at the marriage altar can afford to think that way. Each couple not only believed that they would live blissfully from this day forward, for better or better; they also believed they were the first ones to ever feel this way. Never had there been a beloved like their beloved, never a wedding song like this one, which they believed no other couple had ever chosen. It was the early seventies, and the question I got at almost every wedding rehearsal was, "Can you play 'We've Only Just Begun'?" The couple always looked a little sheepish with the next sentence. They were, after all, a military couple, standing beside the American flag trying to do this right. "We know it's radical, that it's not a standard wedding song, but, well, it's *our* song."

"I'll see what I can do," I'd answer, pretending to search through the stack of books beside me, then feigning surprise as the well-worn sheet music emerged from between the pages of Lohengrin's Bridal March and "O Promise Me." I could have closed my eyes and played the piece from memory, imagining Karen Carpenter's voice sliding over each phrase. Instead I squinted as if seeing the notes for the first time. "I'll try my best," I'd say.

If the couples believed their suggestion was radical, it was nothing compared to their radical faith that the marriage would last. During the seventies, the national odds were one in three, but military couples fared less well. My ringless fingers, spread across the keys, bore witness to this fact. But I kept silent, knowing that nothing I said would make any difference. For the innocents at the altar there is only this moment, and what else can it do but last? I know because I have been there, twice. You have to believe that this is the one that will save you--this ring, this beloved, this blank page unrolling its perfect white promise across your desk. When a famous celebrity was asked, after her seventh wedding or eighth, why she kept trying, she answered, "I believe in marriage." So it is with writers. We believe in the word, the sentence, the poem and the story, particularly the ones we have not yet written. Despite the possibility of failure--the unconsummated couplings or the passionate short-lived trysts or the long-standing unions that wear themselves out--we keep going back to the altar. Maybe this time, maybe this song, maybe this novel. And if it doesn't work out, what else can we do but keep on writing. After all, it's our job.

AUNT

Yesterday we spent the afternoon at the lawyer's office, drawing up our wills. My husband's took only a few minutes. "I'm taking all my parts with me," he said when he got to the organ donor section. "Everything else goes to you, if I die first." *If you survive him*, is the way the lawyer put it. I laughed, thinking of Aunt Bessie. Every morning she'd study the obituaries. "Listen to this," she'd say, smoothing the crease in the newspaper. "Mr. Etheridge is survived by his wife Matilda. Doesn't that just slay you? *Survived by*. Any wife who can survive Bo Etheridge, she deserves to get everything." Then Bessie would get quiet, her eyes again busy on the page, and I'd know she'd spotted a child's obituary. "They're so short," she once said. "Not much to list, I guess."

After an hour my husband shook his head, lifted his hands in surrender. I had been pausing at each line, considering the left eyeball, the right. I want every organ, every possession accounted for. For one niece, the piano and gold pocketwatch. For another, Aunt Bessie's century-old baby shoes, black leather with button clasps. Who will want my diaries, the notebooks, the family-reunion of words collected in my books? My property will be put into a trust to be divided equally for the education of the nephews and nieces. There are fourteen of them, a tribe of borrowed children, mine for the asking. So I ask. One by one I try them on, wear them a day, a week. The best of both worlds, everyone says. Enjoy them, but when you've had enough, send them home where they belong. I think of the fledgling; it is wrong to touch a baby bird, to leave your scent, for when the mother returns to the nest, she will know you have been there.

Maybe some of us were meant from the beginning to be aunts. Maybe we are too weak to bear the full weight of a child. How many times have I had this nightmare--a baby being sucked from my hands out an open window, and me left holding the sack of its nightgown. Maybe the powers-that-be give children to women who can survive the love, who know when to let go, who won't die if they suddenly find themselves holding an empty nightgown. My mother must have known from the start that I would never have children. I needed a guide for that other road, the road my mother had not taken, so she sent for Aunt Bessie.

Bessie was my grandmother's older sister and she arrived on schedule each time my mother gave birth. She wasn't particularly good with babies, but she was available. Grandma had the farm to keep up, chickens and geese and corn and cows and beans and horses to feed. Aunt Bessie was portable. Since she belonged to no one but herself, she could easily pull up stakes and join us for as long as my mother needed her. The way I saw it, she was created solely for our convenience.

The night she arrived to help out with my baby sister, I was sitting cross-legged on my bed, reviewing the events leading up to World War II for the test the next day. When I heard gravel in the driveway, I walked to the window and lifted a slat on the Venetian blinds. Dad was opening the door to the passenger side and from the light of the porch, I saw her emerge. In a few minutes she stood in the doorway of my room holding a brown suitcase, layered like an exiled Jew from the pages of my history book, her navy blue wool coat stuffed so tight that the buttonholes squinted. And as I watched, an amazing thing happened. She started out plump, then sweater by sweater, blouse by blouse, skirt by skirt, she shrunk until she stood before me, a humped scrawny sparrow of a woman in a brown taffeta dress with glittery buttons.

I ran into the kitchen where my mother was stirring a pot of bubbly stew, balancing the baby on her hip. "Why me?" I screamed. Mother just shrugged and smiled, as if that were answer enough.

"Why me? Why not Claudia or Jenny?"

"They're night owls, honey. Aunt Bessie's an early riser like you."

By the third day the battle lines were drawn. I divided the dresser. Lining the mirror on my side was a row of dolls which I dutifully dressed each morning, a three-tiered jewelry box that played "Around the World in Eighty Days," a cache of plastic pop beads and initial bracelets, a pair of clip-on earrings I was not yet allowed to wear, and a grainy five-by-seven of Ricky Nelson which I had scissored from *Teen* magazine. On her side, arranged on a yellowed doily, was everything she had unzipped from the satin pouch of her suitcase--a gold pocketwatch, tweezers, a box of Polident, a framed picture of Lord Byron, a huge black purse with a clamp like an alligator's jaw, and a photograph of a sad young woman. My mother said it was Aunt Bessie's wedding picture, but I didn't believe it. I had seen plenty of wedding pictures--the bride radiant in a flouncy veil and pearls, her white-toothed groom bending over her as they cut the cake together, hand over hand, grinning into the camera.

No, I decided, the woman in this picture could not possibly be a bride. She was standing alone in a shapeless gown. Her head was bare, her hair yanked into a knot--not the silky chignon the women in Wagon Train wore--just a tight thin knot, without ribbon or other adornment. She was turned sideways, her head bent low, and she was holding--not a bridal bouquet with streamers--but one rose, drooping as if it were falling from her hand. My mother assured me there *had* been a husband and that he loved Aunt Bessie so much he built her a home in Stockwell, Indiana, with an oval window embedded in the front door, a home filled with beautiful things, like linen napkins pressed just so in the drawer of a heavy chest that stood in the entry hall. I didn't believe that either. "If Aunt Bessie was really married," I said, "where are the grandchildren?"

"She had one baby," my mother answered. "But it died a long time ago, long before I was born." I could not imagine history that ancient.

By the third week I was wishing Aunt Bessie dead, or at least transported to my sisters' room. I hated her oldness--the swish of taffeta down the hall, the clonk of heavy heels, and the mechanical clack of her loose dentures. Over the years many dentists had tried their best, but Aunt Bessie had a crooked jaw, and when my father finally located a specialist and paid hundreds of dollars for two sets that actually fit, she lost them both--one in a field in Pennsylvania where we'd stopped to pick blackberries and one at sixty-miles-per-hour, in the cubicle bathroom of a Greyhound bus. Finally in desperation my father settled for an economy set. Every night I'd pull the covers over my head and try to sleep as she propped up a pillow, turned on the night light attached to the headboard, and clacked her way through *National Geographic*, Browning's Last Duchess, seed catalogs, fairy tales, detective magazines, *Reader's Digest*, whatever she could find. She always ended with Byron. She didn't read silently with her eyes like normal people, but she didn't exactly read *aloud* either. She simply moved her crooked jaw a little and whispered, just enough movement to set her dentures clacking. That was the last sound I heard at night.

And in the morning I'd wake to the fizz of Polident in a glass by the bed. I'd look up through bleary eyes for my first sight of the day--Aunt Bessie leaning at the waist and pouring her powdery breasts into a stiff brassiere. She'd stand by the mirror and pluck a stray whisker from her chin. This disturbed me: a woman with whiskers. And not only whiskers. All over her body, hair sprouted in unlikely places--from her nostrils, her ears--migrating from the places where I judged it *should* be, the places where it was just beginning on me. She never shaved her legs, yet they were smooth as the legs of my rubber dolls. The pits of her underarms were hairless. Even her eyebrows were missing. She'd sketch them in each morning with a small black pencil that she kept rolled in a hankie. "Old maid," I'd hiss beneath the covers. Then when she was gone, swishing down the hall, I'd crawl from bed and dress for school, where girls with real eyebrows were gathering in the halls.

I had long since given up my dolls, but every Sunday I volunteered to dress Aunt Bessie for church. She was the only grownup small enough and old enough to be under my control. Looking back, I wonder why she let me use her.

Maybe she liked the attention. Maybe the feel of young hands was so comforting that she bore the humiliation.

I started with her hair. It was gray, but not the silver floss of my grandmother nor the spongy blue-gray of widows whose hair is constructed each Saturday morning. Hers was the muddied gray of leftover snow. She'd lean over the kitchen sink and I'd lather up the Prell. Wet, her hair was fine as a baby's. Her scalp beneath my fingers was pink and exposed, and I could hardly stand to look at it. I'd squeeze the wet hair into a towel, then coerce a rattail comb through, making parts for the yellow rollers--a row down the center from her forehead to the nape of her neck. Then pincurls on each side, above her ears.

It was the year of dryer bonnets--my mother had gotten one for Christmas--so next she would be put under. I'd slide the plastic daisy bonnet onto her head and it would fall toward her eyes, over the scratchings of what was left of her eyebrows, their shapely arches having long since swirled down the drain with the Prell. I'd set the timer for ten minutes. With each minute, her face reddened and chapped and she talked louder and louder as if it were *my* ears that were covered. When the timer went off, I unrolled the curlers one by one and for a minute she was a Shirley Temple doll, the ringlets tight and shiny from the heat. Then the artistry, the teasing and back-combing at the crown to give her the fullness I'd seen in *Ladies Home Journal*. Then two curls on either side of her forehead, swirling inward like a ram's horns. "Cover your eyes!" I'd shout, and her hands would jump to her face while I sprayed Aqua Net until she choked and begged "No More!" I'd pat her hair, shoot one final spray, and she would smile. A little blush on her cheeks, a little pink lipstick. She'd replace the eyebrows herself while I held the mirror.

Her hands were strong and fearsome, her yellowed nails like talons curving in. The manicure was the final challenge: the taming of a wild thing. First I clipped the thick nails, then filed them into ovals. I rubbed cream into her hands and fingers. Her skin was thin, stretched over knuckles knotty as roots, nothing left but bone and gristle. I'd choose Avon, some childish pink or coral, and begin painting the nails. Two coats. Blow on them to dry. And then the dress. The black crepe or the navy blue taffeta? Maybe the white blouse with a cameo pin. I chose for this Sunday a flowery chintz my mother had made--pale green with yellow zinnias and a ruffled lace collar. "Fine," she said, and I slipped the dress over her head, over the safety-pinned strap of her brassiere and past her crooked hip. I zipped up the back and she was done.

I grew three inches that year, sailing past Aunt Bessie's lopsided shoulders. The waistbands of my dresses rose while my underwear slid below my belly button, and saddle shoes that were fine one afternoon pinched my toes the next morning. I was Alice in Wonderland, a fever dream pulsing out of control. It didn't surprise my mother. "Kids grow at night," she said matter-of-factly. "That's why they wake up hungry. It's hard work."

One night a few months later I woke with excruciating pain in my calves, as if my legs were being stretched on a rack. I kicked off the covers and grabbed my knees, pulling my calves in close. The night light switched on above my head and Aunt Bessie was up, turning her face toward me. She was a drawing pad sketch, a gesture, a jot, the mere suggestion of a face. Eyebrows, teeth, the hair-sprayed pouf of morning hair, were missing. All that remained were her eyes, dark sockets that loomed huge and black without the softening frame of glasses.

She sighed a self-satisfied sigh, as if she'd been anticipating this moment all her life. "Growing pains," was all she said, yet even that was garbled, delivered, as it was, toothless. She creaked from her side of the bed and walked in the semi-darkness to my side. She rubbed her arthritic hands together. Carefully she folded back the covers and touched my shoulder, coaxing me to turn. Then she rummaged in the headboard shelf and I smelled wintergreen as she squeezed Ben-Gay onto her hands.

Why I gave in so easily, I still don't know. In daylight she was the last person I wanted, the last person I would have imagined touching me. I could have called for my mother; she surely would have come. But I was helpless in the pain and confusion of this newest trick my body was playing, and Aunt Bessie's hands went right for the hurting place. They kneaded and rubbed and tamed the pulsing muscles of my calves. Her yellowed knotted hands, the protruding veins, the fingernails I'd painted orange just that morning. She squeezed more ointment from the tube, warmed it between her palms, and began to rub my calves again. Finally the pain stopped. My tears stopped. And for the moment, at least, I stopped growing.

Nights when my husband is working, I drive across town to see my niece, delighting in the small hands running a brush through my hair or slapping red polish on my nails. "Walk on my back," I say, so I can feel her plump feet kneading the kinks. Sometimes at night I crawl into my nephew's bed and curl behind him, press into his warm back and touch his chest, feeling the heartbeat, holding my next breath until I feel *his*. Yesterday my niece called me into the bathroom to read her a "potty story" while she sat on the toilet. Her pudgy hands gripped the rim so she wouldn't fall in, and her training pants had slid to her feet. As I looked down, the skin of her thighs was translucent. Beneath it ran a fine river of blue vein. And last month when my nephew turned two, the outside world found him. It landed in dirt creases on the back of his neck. While I wasn't looking, he learned to sweat, and now instead of the powdery baby scent, his smell is the smell of a wet puppy.

This past summer I turned forty two. On my birthday, my mother sent a leather diary marked 1897. It is Aunt Bessie's diary. In it are recorded the small moments of her seventeenth year. The handwriting is eccentric and unpredictable as she was, at times painstaking in its perfection, at other times scrawling and nearly illegible. There are entries of anger and self-pity, loneliness and disappointment, then sudden wild-geese flights of joy. She wishes for the words to come more easily. She longs for the power to express the sting of a sleighride, the red burn of sunset, the taste of oyster soup and apples.

Usually she borrows the words of others, Longfellow and Byron mostly, only occasionally breaking into songs of her own, recalling the gleam of sun on a field "ridged with frost" or a sky "cloudless except for a few fleecy ones in the east." And as I read the diary, it begins to make sense--my hunger for words, my very choice of vocation. I want to thank her, but she is not here.

The night nurse said she would call for us, the grandnieces and nephews, her voice down the hospital corridor unrolling our many names, beginning and ending with mine. She died alone, between shifts. A stranger dressed her and parted her hair and brushed rouge across her gray cheeks. She was buried on a muddy March afternoon, just a few miles from her birthplace. Now all these years later I hold her to me--a tribal instinct perhaps, to know our mother's sister, our father's sister, the sister of our grandmother. The bond without the bind. Or perhaps I simply want to give back some of the words to the young woman in the diary. I sit in my study where shelves of books line the green walls. I finger the dictionaries and search for what lies beneath: Aunt. From old French, *ante*, an offshoot, hall leading toward the main room. Latin root, *amma*: Mother. Or *amare*: to love. As in *amigo*, as in *amour*. As in *amateur*, one who works for the bare love of it.

COMPOSTING: NOTES FROM A WRITER'S JOURNAL

Not long after my second book came out, a reviewer sent a list of questions to help me prepare for a telephone interview. A typographical error had translated his final question into "What is your theory of *composting*?" I thought it was a wonderful question; it seemed more than mere coincidence that only one letter separates "composing" from "composting." A gardener saves everything organic--apple peelings, leaves, eggshells, coffee grounds; tosses them out back; allows the mixture to breed awhile, rot awhile; turns it occasionally with a pitchfork, stirring up stored heat; and finally, works the rich mulch into the depleted soil, where new vegetables sprout the following summer.

For many years I have kept a journal filled with scraps of daily wonderings, newspaper clippings, quotes, unsent love letters, drafts of poems and stories, unsent hate letters, maps, sketches, song lyrics, and details of my personal life. At times I've questioned the value of this undertaking, and as I've reread certain entries, I've questioned the wisdom of saving it all. Leaning over the fence, my neighbor says, "My mother taught me never to write down anything I wouldn't want to be used against me in court." I understand her reasoning; I have, in fact, burned several journals recently. Yet still I remain a believer in writing it all down, even if it will later be tossed into the fire. Certainly most of what a writer records in a journal is for private use only. However, I've always loved reading the informal jottings of other writers; it especially thrills me to read of their struggles and failures, so much like my own. The following journal entries cover a ten-year period. Taken together, they begin to define my working definition of the composing, or composting process.

*****

Looking down at the blank page, I wonder if we ever

unlearn the fear. It's the same dizziness I used to experience while standing on the edge of the high dive and staring down into the water. So many fears met in this moment, tying themselves into a knot at the center of my stomach. First, the simple childhood fear that I would twist the wrong way, fall to the concrete, and never rise again. Then, the fear of the plunge, that mid-air flight between the hard reality of the board and the release into icy water--those few seconds when I was suspended, attached to nothing, sailing out of control. And was there yet another fear, one that has taken me all these years to see? The fear that I would disturb something so blue and whole, that I would enter its stillness like an alien bullet, ruffling the surface and shaking loose the quiet world beneath. Let's say I have a memory, strong and alive, a memory so rich I could dream it again and again and its color would never completely wash over me. Naturally I want to keep it forever. So I plunge--with my words that stumble, the awkward crossings-out, my graceless misunderstandings--and suddenly that memory has become something else. Like the blue unruffled water beneath me, it will never be the same once I have made the plunge. Is that why it took me six years to write the grandmother poem?

*****

Writing feels impossible, each word the move of Sisyphus. My stories are lackluster; they stare back at me with that look on their faces. "So what?" they say. Nothing I write feels earned or necessary. I'm just putting in time, yet I'm afraid to stop and simply wait for the work to ripen on its own, afraid I will lose it completely. All I want is to find the pulse, what I *must* write, but my mind is like a pinball machine with thousands of possibilities bouncing off at once, and I can't hold onto any of them long enough. I am not able to be the ox that Barry Hannah says a writer must be; I cannot see with tunnel vision, plod the straightest path through a piece of work. How did my other poems and stories come, as if unbidden? Strange to look back at my best pieces and not be able to recall how they were engendered. I woke this morning with these words in my head: "I am the rooster who has forgotten how. You are morning, caught in my throat." Is this the writer, speaking to the work?

* * * * *

Walking at midday, a fear overcame me--that the words that have always fed me would flee, never to return. In a recent interview, Edna O'Brien talked about the underground springs in Ireland that suddenly dry up; yet often, when the water-diviners come, they find another spring. She said that as artists, we must learn to be our own water-diviners. Maybe this is the hardest task of all--to trust that another spring will be found. In the meantime, what do we do? Do I try, as Marge Piercy says, to squeeze poems "out of the absolute zero/of my night"? Or do I dumbly wait, like a fallow field? When I'm not feeling generous, when I don't feel I have anything to give back to the world--should I even try to write? My poet friend tells me he writes less and less now, recognizing he must be in just the right "space" to produce anything decent. Perhaps writers are different that way--maybe I need to write a thousand words before I get two phrases that surprise me. Do poems grow within us slowly, taking root until they spring fullgrown from our pens, like Athena from Zeus's head? Or does the ink itself, as it flows, begin the process of their birth? How much do we push? And how do we know when there is something alive waiting to be born?

Rilke speaks of the "listening blue" in Cezanne's still lifes and landscapes, the blue which encompasses and "listens to" the bright primary reds and yellows. I think of writers as this listening blue, mediating between the work and the audience, helping birth the truth of what must be said, yet waiting for signs, not pushing what must be said or trying to put words into the mouth of the work. The form informs the words; the words inform the form. It is all one, and the artist must live in this uneasy state of receptor and maker, all in the same breath. No wonder truth is so hard to capture, for it forms itself within the materials and within the processes of the work itself. Maybe my job as a writer is to keep one ear to the ground to listen for the work to speak.

*****

I am feeling again the stupid courage necessary to plunge back into the novel, to start fresh and see where it will take me. But I am also terrified, partly because I will have to throw away even more than I already have, which feels like waste to me. Intellectually I know nothing is ever wasted, but emotionally I am not so sure. What will become of the failed chapters, the years of work? I've written the novel twice already. Do I have the energy to carry it through one more time? Of course, no one can answer the question except myself; no one will keep me going except myself.

*****

Yesterday a colleague's wife committed suicide. She was thirty-nine years old--wife, mother, successful businesswoman "with everything," the newspaper account assures us, "going for her." Is this why she killed herself? Was there *too* much going for her, against her?

On my walk this evening I look inside lighted houses where everything appears so cool and clean, every knick-knack in place. Two doors down, a woman is on her knees scrubbing her walkway with Clorox. Its scent follows me like a homeless dog, and I think of all I've left undone--the dust piling up, the dirt I've swept under rugs, the unpolished shoes I've stashed in the backs of closets. On my September calendar is a painting by a Dutch woman who was prolific and successful with her art all her life. At twenty-nine she married, had "ten surviving children," and as her biographer notes, "her domestic life never interrupted her activities as a painter." Why does this depress me, make me feel small, like Metis swallowed by Zeus? I demand the truth. How many servants did this artist have? Where did she send her children? Who shopped for food, cooked it, held her children's heads when they were sick? We do not need more models of women artists who have done it all. We need permission to say No to some things so that we can say Yes to our work. My teacher Audre Lorde once told me, "It is hard to fight an enemy who has outposts in your head." I am exhausted from my own inner cheerleader: "Yes you can do it all. Yes, yes, yes." No, I can't, and I must remember this. Perhaps our greatest untapped strength lies in welcoming failure in some parts of our lives in order to free up space for what is important. We need to talk to each other, break open the silences, so that no more women kill themselves on our newspaper pages--saying Yes to everything except their lives.

* * * * *

Insult to injury: my work comes back from the editors *postage due*. The ransom of red poem. A trip to the post office to retrieve the bad boy held hostage so long, I'd forgotten his name. Did he bite too hard? More likely he whined until his keepers, weary of his face, finally screamed, "Back to your mother!" and pointed to the door.

* * * * *

A writer is nothing when she is not writing. Even a week away from the words leaves me sullen, but I do not realize it until I stop for a minute, the dust dies down, and I see that nothing--not this crisp April morning, the light on the multi-colored grass, or the lovely cliché of my neighbor's white picket fence--is enough. Nothing satisfies like the words coming together, the making of a new poem. Sometimes I wish I were different, wish I were able to live contentedly without this compulsive need for work--and occasionally, for brief moments, I am. Music lifts me and my life makes sense. I notice the stem of the peony in the vase, the candles that Donald has lit for dinner, green napkins against a lace tablecloth, the pink shrimp and the bottle of wine. I can live awhile on this moment, but it does not last; always, I must grope my way back to the words. It is only when I am in the midst of a project, writing something which pulls me to the desk each day, that I can truly hold the beauty around me. To be denied writing would throw me into despair.

It's five a.m., and I'm sitting beside my niece's bed, watching her sleep and trying to scribble myself into wakefulness. An envelope of light opens across her hair. Oh, to be the sleeper awash in this sea of comfort--a quilt around my shoulders, the slow lift and fall of my chest. Then to wake lazily, move in slippers through a quiet house, taking my time. Instead I am the watcher, taking notes. Is it some weakness, inherited, to need the words this much?

*****

"The plot thickens." Yes, if only a novel were like pudding--once it thickens, it's done. And nourishing. And pronounced delicious by all who eat it. Unfortunately, it is not that way. Does it ever get easier? Now that I'm caught in the middle of the process, it seems more mysterious, more difficult than ever. How does a book ever get written?

I cannot let myself think, "This must be good." Thinking this way paralyzes me. The little gremlins in the back of my mind mock me, making it hard to focus, to trust, to allow the connections to emerge on their own. I must give myself permission--no, encouragement!--to write badly.

*****

At last night's reading, I was again reminded that literature must move us to a new place or it is worthless. Cleverness is never enough. So the reader's story was not enough for me, although it was filled with irony and word-play that made the audience laugh. Finally it came down to: who cares about a stove? Even had the stove been granted human characteristics, I doubt that I would have cared, for the story was treated with no tenderness, no love. Great writers can make us love almost anything. When I read Neruda, it's his sympathy for all pieces of life--insects and animals and flowers--that opens my heart to his words. His love and the unstopping passion to get inside each leaf, each dog's ear--to learn not its secrets or answers, but the mystery of its shadow. And he is so generous with himself, using the "I" not in a blindly-confessional way like Plath or Sexton, but in such a self-effacing yet honest way that I believe him totally. I laugh aloud at his "Another Dog" poem in which he follows a dog in the streets in order to learn "where dogs go/in their tour of night." But the laughter that springs from me feels richer, more earned, than the kind I heard at the reading last night.

So I went home from the reading and got out the drafts I have been working on, remembering a quote from Einstein: "Everything should be made as simple as possible, but not simpler." Now I see these drafts are unsatisfactory because they do not explore the complexities of the question. They are too simple, the anger too easily directed; in their neatness, their tied-up-with-a-bow endings, they fall short of art. I must test and re-test the work until it brings me to a new set of questions or a new level of emotion.

*****

Reading William Goyen's stories and interviews always opens uncharted places for me, so I reread his notes about the difference between creative and destructive memory. He says he must now flee the "dark angel" when he feels it coming, that he must not be afraid of the dark side, but realize that true art must be, finally, a healing. This is comforting to me, for I want my work to move in that direction. To stop with raw pain is not enough. It must be filtered, distilled into something finer; yet without the initial pain, there is no joy, only a shallow smile that has not earned itself. His theory that art is, finally, a healing, is one I agree with--but this healing cannot be a quick fix, a happy ending tacked on to tie up loose ends. It must take place within the inner eye of each reader, each participator in the work. The work need not show this process overtly; rather, the work must be written in such a way that the reader can experience the despair and the subsequent healing for himself. There might be a step in the process which feels like pain, which feels like despair--but it cannot stop there. Yesterday, while reading *The Book of Nightmares*, I emerged on the other side of the pain. Although Kinnell's images are dark and disturbing, at the end of the tunnel it is *love* that reigns. I am renewed: made new again. In the midst of the horror and nightmare, human love is not only possible, but necessary.

In much contemporary poetry, I see ranting and raving, mere self-indulgent pain, and that is not art any more than vomiting or bleeding or pissing on canvas is art. Yes, I have been moved by works that contain much ugliness, even despair. Yet finally I believe that art must not only break our hearts, but heal the break, all in one sweep. I want my writing to give something back to the world, something that transfigures the ease of anger and blame and acknowledges that place where sometimes I arrive, by accident or blessing--not memory, exactly, but a place between first memory and now. I want to catch that feeling before it flutters away. To live on the edge of that possibility would be to truly live.

*****

Rabbit has been gone for three days. Donald says not to worry, that it's just what cats do. Rabbit has always come back before, he reminds me. Still, each morning I go to the front door and begin my search, forgetting for a moment that cats, like poems, don't come when you call.

*****

My book will be out any day now. A year late, and at times I feel the poems are not mine anymore, but written from some other hand. I'm always closest to what I'm working on now--so much so that the old poems are almost an embarrassment. Linda Pastan says we should not compare one of our poems, or one book, to another. "Is my third child better than my first child?" she asks. I've heard many writers say that the publication of a book is like giving birth. For me, it was seven years' gestation (writing the poems) and two years of delivering the book into the hands of the publishers. Now others will see my child. First I'll check for the obvious: Does she have all her fingers, her toes? Is there a heartbeat? Only later will I begin to fear what others might think. Has she inherited my clear eyes, my good skin? What if, instead, she's inherited my cowlicks that won't lie flat, my narrow shoulders, the veiny thighs? Still, I believe I will love her, even if she appears with ears that I swear could not possibly be mine. Of course I will love her--my own red-faced, squalling, perfectly imperfect child.

*****

I need to dig deeper into my work. I've been dancing around the edges of it, trying to fit it into my tight schedule. Yesterday, exhausted after a day of teaching, I hurried to my desk, thinking that I would jump right back into the new poem. Of course I failed. Poems cannot be jumped into like a pile of leaves, or written in installments. When I try to do it this way, the price is heavy. I feel my writing calling, begging for more attention.

*****

I've spent two days and all night, around the clock, rereading the disparate pieces of the novel and trying to dream them into some whole. An efficiency expert would wring his hands at the waste this effort represents. Four years of writing, reshaping, hearing criticism, typing, editing, more reshaping, and now I'm down again to the bare bones of the story I must tell. It occurs to me how much still needs to go, and how much yet waits to be written.

*****

An exhilarating morning in the library reading about the lives of chickens and roosters, and about the birthing of cows. I love facts. The world is so large and fascinating that I could read day in and night out, and not begin to touch the mysteries. If someone would pay my bills, I would gladly read for a living. Yes, as long as I think of myself as a reader, I am joyous; library shelves glow with amber light and the books (thousands and thousands of books!) wrap themselves around me.

But when it's time to write, I shiver, caught in the shadows of other writers. My pen squeezes out each word, like blood the nurse smears on the slide. How can I write a poem about wives and mistresses when Sexton has done it so well? And pain? What do I know of pain? Reading Sharon Olds, my measly pain slips back into its hole while hers pulses from the page, as if she had pushed the words so hard the wristbones split with the force. My pain will never be as bright as hers, will never burst, then petal into words as fine. On the wall behind me is Kundera's *The Unbearable Lightness of Being*, a book almost too beautiful to bear. How was he able to weave private love stories with public political questions, and make such a durable cloth? Yesterday I spent four hours trying to move one character from the refrigerator to the bed. At times like this I feel like one of those cartoon characters who gets dropped onto a conveyor belt and plops out the other end--alive, yet squished into the shape of a box, all the features intact yet rearranged.

Toni Morrison's *Sula* is at my elbow; I pick it up. Each sentence is rich and authentic, and I immediately begin to wish I could write with that kind of voice. Then it occurs to me: her voice would not sound authentic coming from my throat, just as my voice could not come from hers. It is so difficult to trust our own voices, to feel we have anything to say. I must remind myself that the importance of any work of art lies not only in the effect it might have on some imagined reader, but also in the impulse, the necessity from which it springs. Though it must finally be honed and tested and crafted for another's ear or eye, it is nothing if it does not flow from that original impulse.

*****

My father has had a heart attack. Over the phone he says that he has one chance in four of living five more years, unless he has the valve operation. "But it's very serious," he says. "I might not make it." He asks me to pray for him. How do I tell him I don't pray anymore, if praying is eyes closing, mouth opening on Jesus' name? Simone Weil said, "Absolute attention is prayer." So this morning, alone in my old robe, I worship the beauty of this quiet--leaves caught on neighbors' roofs, the dark rotting of branches fallen into gutters. Gray trees, gray housetops, silver-gray sky. I read poems and gasp at the holiness of words--the linking and coupling, then the breaking apart as a new line forms and each word begins again its solitary life. Rilke said that art is "the knot in the rosary at which his life recites a prayer."

I sit alone and write these lines, anxious to pile one upon the other until the page is full. Thinking of my father, I worry that words will not find their partners, that a sentence will begin and trail off, unravel before my eyes. It is a pleasure simple and complete to watch each word connect, attach itself to the next. Each line I write, assurance. Meaning grows on the page. Each push of the pen, a prayer.

*****

I have never felt happier, more alive. Nothing frightens me in moments like these. Yesterday I broke my two-month silence and wrote a poem, which grew and grew until now I see it wants to become a whole series of poems--"The Brides of Zeus" or perhaps "The Wives of Zeus." I must guard my time, for writing is the center of all that I am. It keeps me from dissolving into reruns of myself; it forces me to re-invent myself each time I go back to the desk. This morning, the "donor" poem finally turned on me, revealing its true self. Isn't this what every writer hopes for--an insurrection, her own words rising up, telling secrets on her? I could live forever in this moment, focussed on the world of the task. What a glorious feeling! Again it comes back to that first place: writing itself is the work, the joy, the reward. All else, as my friend Agnes says, is Chinese boxes.

Here's another small victory, a first for me. A "No" came in the mail this afternoon and, for the first time, I did not feel hurt. Instead, while filing the note with all the others I've accumulated over the years, I crossed out the folder label marked "Rejections" and renamed it "Free to Send Out." I am so happy to be writing poems again that, for now, I don't really care if anyone wants them.

*****

Finally, after a lingering illness, the novel has died in my arms. Every time I tried to breathe life into it, I failed. It's time to bury it. As Suzanne says, maybe I began it in another life. Yet this possibility also exists: that while this particular spring has dried up, another will one day be discovered nearby, fed from the same underground stream. Last night I read this quote by a sculptor, and I reread it now for comfort: "You hang a picture, execute a painting and shoot a photograph--It implies that to make something new, something has to be altered or destroyed."

On the phone, Suzanne tells me about her daughter, who has been nursing her first child for nearly two years. Now that her daughter is pregnant again, however, the breast milk has turned bitter. It's time to wean the first child in order to prepare for the second.

*****

When I read Seamus Heaney, his poems enter through a place more primal than mere understanding. His is not an overlay of language, but rather an underneath-river-of-language so deep that he renames the world even as he re-sees it. I love the look of his words; no one else puts them together in the same way. And when I read the words, even silently, it feels as if something is suddenly loose and warm in my mouth, something more than tongue, some rich broth or cream of language. In his bog poems, the traveling is thick. It takes my tongue a while to complete its journey, step by step. As if trudging in heavy boots, I lift each word, each syllable, from the sucking mud. In other poems, like the one about his mother, the words are fine as dust collecting, or flour--the talcum of memory sifting softly. I am sad for anyone who has not traveled the language of his poems.

* * * * *

Last night we watched a television interview with José Carreras, who is in remission from the leukemia that almost killed him. "The illness changed me," he said. "Now, I sing because it is a privilege to sing." Although the doctors had warned him against using his voice while he was in treatment, he could not help himself. I imagine him singing--through the drip of chemotherapy, while his hair is falling out in handfuls--simply for the joy of singing. This famous tenor, who has performed in the most prestigious opera houses in the world, now says that his favorite place to sing is his own bathroom. There's nothing like the resonance from my own shower, he says. Better than Carnegie Hall. My friend, a novelist, tells me he doesn't believe a word of it; no one sings, no one writes, no one paints, just for the privilege of it. We sing, he says, in order to be heard. This thought comes to me: if a writer sings in the forest, and there's no one else to hear, does she make any sound?

* * * * *

I've just completed a poetry lesson with twenty-seven children, and now it's time to write. Usually I circulate to help, but lately I've felt like a beginner and I'm hoping that if I watch long enough, I'll remember what to do. I squeeze myself into a tiny wooden desk and wait to see what will happen. How do twenty-seven eight-year-olds approach the task of writing a poem? Here is what I see:

They move their mouths silently, they hesitate, blow eraser dust away, lean on one elbow, talk to the air, nudge their neighbor, smile, scratch their heads, whisk the erasures with the heel of their hand, put their tongues between their teeth, chew on their erasers, wonder, hum, point, peek at their neighbor's paper, make their own space, sniff their pencils, suck their fingers, lean on the other elbow, peek at their neighbor's paper again, cry, laugh, thump their shoes, twirl their hair around their fingers, bite their thumbnails, push their glasses onto their noses, bear down so hard on their pencils they leave imprints on their notebook pad, clasp their hands tightly as if in prayer until their knuckles are white.

In other words, they act the same way I do when trying to enter that mysterious place where poems are planted, except for them it's more difficult. I think of that old joke about Ginger Rogers: She did everything Fred Astaire did, only she did it backwards and in heels. This little boy beside me is doing the same things I do in my study, only he's doing it in a hard wooden desk, surrounded by twenty-six other hard-breathing strugglers, while the gerbil is squeaking in its cage and the intercom is hissing its afternoon pronouncements. If he can do it, so can I. I take my pen from my pocket and begin.

* * * * *

Michelangelo believed the statues he sculpted were already hidden inside the marble. He could not quite visualize the figure, but he knew it was only a matter of chipping away the surface. So this morning at my desk, while I was attending to a different task, the excess marble fell away and I saw the shape of my novel. Its name will be *The Riddle Song*, and it will have twelve parts. Full grown, it will be one third the size of its mother, the dead novel. It is all so clear to me now, after all the years of labor, after I had given up. This must be the creative hatching that Einstein described: "Kieks--auf einmal ist es da!" Cheep--and all at once there it is.

*****

I am studying a still life of lutes, violins, flutes and horns leaning against an old music stand, with a half-burned candle on the side. The colors, too, are burnt and dark, but light is reflecting warm and radiantly from some hidden source--a window perhaps, not shown in the picture. The beauty our eyes behold is caused not always by what shows, but also by those unseen presences that cause a reflection. Painters say they do not wait for inspiration; they simply follow the light. My cat Rabbit finds the one patch of sunlight in the house and lies in the middle of it. When the light moves, he follows it room to room, basting himself in its warmth. I'm remembering the poem the little boy wrote in class last week: "Glow is when your cat falls asleep inside a sunbeam." It is difficult for me to keep relearning this lesson--of following the light where it leads, of trusting to something as yet unseen. My cat finds warmth in the middle of January. One small strip of sun is enough.

WORKS CITED

Einstein, Albert, quoted in *Reader's Digest*, October 1977.

Heaney, Seamus, *Selected Poems 1966-1987*, New York: Farrar Straus & Giroux, 1991.

Kinnell, Galway, *The Book of Nightmares*, New York: Houghton Mifflin, 1971.

Kundera, Milan, *The Unbearable Lightness of Being*, New York: Harper and Row, 1984.

Morrison, Toni, *Sula*, New York: Knopf, 1974.

Neruda, Pablo, *New Poems (1968-1970)*, New York: Grove Press, 1972.

O'Brien, Edna, Interview in *Paris Review*, No. 92, Summer 1984.

Olds, Sharon, *The Dead and the Living*, New York: Knopf, 1975.

Piercy, Marge, *Circles on the Water: Selected Poems of Marge Piercy*, New York: Knopf, 1982.

Rilke, Rainer Maria, *Letters on Cezanne*, Translated by Joel Agee, New York: Fromm International Publishing Corporation, 1985.

Sexton, Anne, *The Complete Poems*, Boston: Houghton Mifflin Company, 1981.

HATCHING

Seventy years later and she still smells it in her dreams. She is my father's oldest sister, and she tells me this over lunch at an uptown department store in her midwestern city where I have come to visit, hungry for something I am afraid will get lost. Last month she had a triple-bypass. Under the designer pantsuit, she is stitched from breastbone to navel and, again, from groin to ankle where they stripped the vein that would feed her heart. It's not the family tree I seek, not the official line a genealogist is paid to trace. What I need are the small moments, the details, the stories aborted that never found their climax, their dénouement. Rag-tags of faded dresses, like pieces my grandmother salvaged and stitched together for quilts. Maybe if I listen hard enough, the scraps will come together. And if the quilt is not beautiful, at least it will be warm, something to throw around my shoulders late at night.

The smell in her dreams is the smell of warm eggs from an incubator that was kept in the bedroom she shared with four sisters. The eggs were in a covered tray with a light bulb hung above for warmth. They were turned once a day. Over the next weeks, one by one the chicks hatched. Usually the girls were asleep when this happened. Sometime in the night an egg would break, a wet chick nudge its head through the shell. Hens are born with thousands of tiny germ cells, each one a potential egg. And each of my aunts was born with 400,000 ova. When the girls got older, they probably all bled at the same time each month. That is what happens, scientists say, when women live together. Five daughters swimming under the same moon. Imagine. No wonder my grandfather often slept under the stars after a day of haying. Two days ago, I visited my father and took a walk with him. "My warranty's run out," he said, laughing but not really laughing. His heart operation six years ago was more serious than my aunt's, and the plastic valve was guaranteed only for five years. Walking with him, I tried hard not to think about this, so hard that I *did* forget for a minute and walked too fast until I heard my father's valve clicking. The love and fear rose in my throat, decades of words that I should have spoken, but didn't.

My aunt is seventy-seven years old but still beautiful and somewhat vain. She wears a scarf at her neck to hide the wrinkles. Once she was a model and she is still tall and graceful. "Always wear shoes that match your stockings and skirt," she says. "That is the key." If my father had been a woman, he would have been my aunt. Maybe this is why I have come; she is as close as I can get to knowing him. I see my father's chin in her chin, his nervous hands in the flutter of her hands straightening a pleat or refolding the napkin, his eyes in her eyes when she looks away, unable to stay grounded in the moment. I do the same thing. Even as she speaks--now she's finished with the incubator and is on to the caul--I am jotting it all in my brain. The moment is never enough for me. I am never wholly there. I justify this unattractive trait with the fact that I am a writer. Every experience is material, I tell myself.

The waiter has brought our chicken salad, served on lettuce ruffled like a doily. My aunt has become very talkative and I take advantage of it. "I don't know how much of this is true," she says like a little boy relishing a naughty joke he's been warned not to repeat, so of course I lean forward. "Your grandma had a sister. Aunt Ceel. She was born in a veil." My aunt says veil but I translate it as caul because I have learned more from books than from life and this is what books call the membrane that wraps the heads of some babies. I should use my aunt's word. It is more beautiful and more mysterious. "So she had powers," my aunt continues. "Plus she was the seventh daughter of a seventh daughter, so she could see things other people couldn't. That's how your grandma first knew she would marry your grandpa. Grandma and Ceel were sitting together in the outhouse, a two-seater. Grandma was sixteen, Ceel much younger, maybe ten or eleven. Suddenly Ceel said that a man was on the road and he was the man your grandma would marry."

As it turned out, my future grandfather *was* the stranger on that road, arriving with a team of horses. It strikes me as ludicrous that this is how my pristine father was engendered, that the romance between my grandparents began in an outhouse, foreseen in the crystal of a young girl's eyes, a great-aunt I would never know. I don't say this to my aunt because I am afraid she will take it wrong. There is something solemn in her expression. Perhaps to her also, this moment is more than this moment. We aren't just an elderly aunt and a fortyish niece eating chicken salad in a department store restaurant; something is being written here. *All these bits,* she seems to say. *They matter. Don't let them die.*

This is my justification for prying. Because of course it finally comes around to sex, and the discussion of sex across generations is always prying. I don't ask for the information directly. It starts as a research question, generic, something an interviewer on a talk show might ask. "I heard you and Grandma were midwives, that you helped other farm women with their babies." This is what my father once told me and it seems a harmless question, but by the time she finishes answering, I will know more than I ever wanted to know.

Because it wasn't quite like that. I should have guessed. How could my father have known what went on in the birthing room? He was a young man, out in the fields with my grandfather and the other sons, but already plotting his escape from the farm. Later he would father nine children, two of whom would die in the womb and one as an infant. Six of us would live, but he would not be present at our births. It was not his fault. In those days, men simply weren't present. They paced in waiting rooms, walking the edges, the perimeters that marked the women's place. My father did the best he could, but the closest he ever got to the blood of it was when my mother was pregnant with my sister and almost hemorrhaged to death. He didn't know I was watching, but I was eleven and curious and afraid he was holding something back from me, that maybe my mother was dead, not safe in a hospital miles away. So I stood at the bathroom door and watched him kneel beside the tub, sloshing her blood-drenched nightgown in the water which was quickly staining to pink.

This is what I'm remembering as my aunt begins the story. "No," she says. "I only helped with one birth. Jack's." Jack is her brother, two years younger than my father. My aunt was seventeen and still living on the farm, the year before she left for the city and a job. Grandma's labor started earlier than expected, earlier and faster, too fast for the family doctor to get there. I am trying to imagine this--watching your own mother give birth, delivering your own brother. There are lines that we draw and this is one I have trouble leaping. I have come close, but not that close. I was present at the birth of my nephew. I held my sister's hands and looked into her wild eyes and calmed her when she screamed that this was a bad idea, that she wasn't going to finish this, that the baby was tearing her apart, was killing her. But a doctor was there, wheeling around on a low stool, taking charge.

My aunt says she doesn't remember much, just helping Grandma onto the dining room table and hearing the screams and seeing the blood, all that blood. Maybe my aunt's head was so filled with hate there was no room for storing the memory. "Hate for Dad," she says, for she had decided at the moment Jack was born that this was all her father's fault, that she hated men and that she would never have children. Never.

"But we knew nothing back then," she says, and suddenly it spills out, something even women who might *think it* will never admit aloud--that her two children, the parents of those smiling grandchildren whose pictures flank her television set--were accidents. I have suspected this all along, for in this, my aunt and I are the same: we like our lives well ordered and under control. You can see this in the careful way we dress, the schedules we keep, our early to bed, early to rise, one-a-day-vitamin mentality. Which is probably why I never had children. Sometimes, mostly in dreams, my body mourns what never was--those 400,000 ova floating unfinished--but most of the time I live in my head, not my body. This is my father in me, not my mother. And it is my aunt. If my aunt had been I, she would have been childless. And if I had been my aunt, married early in the days before The Pill, I would have been the one with two accidents. I would have been the one laid out on that same dining room table where three years before she had watched her mother give birth.

Yes, this is the real story, the one that finally breaks it all open and hatches the fear inside my head: Fifty-seven years ago in Illinois there was a blizzard. This is not exactly the way my aunt tells it, but I am doing the math in my head as she speaks. She was barely twenty, married less than a year and living out her pregnancy. Because, short of killing yourself, there is no way out of this contract. The baby *will* come. She had been visiting her parents and because of the blizzard, her husband could not get to her. "Or wouldn't," she says, after all these years still not sure. The doctor had been notified, but it was doubtful he would make it. When the contractions started, Grandma helped her onto the table. For two nights and three days she was in labor. Outside the dining room, Grandpa walked the floors, stomping and cursing, knowing that if no one else arrived, he would have to help. He had never been this close to the birthing room before and if he hadn't thought his daughter might die, he wouldn't have been this close now.

At the last minute the doctor arrived with ether, but he couldn't give her much. Grandma couldn't hold my aunt down by herself, so Grandpa was forced to help. The doctor finally pulled the baby out of her. It took eleven stitches to sew her up. "I felt every one," she says. Her father was holding her head, his rough farmer hands tight on her temples. When it was over she looked up to him and, "as hateful as ever I said anything," she says, and her teeth clench on the memory, "I said 'You did this to Mother too.'" Later Grandma told her the dining room had looked as if a hog had been butchered there.

When my aunt finishes the story, her eyes are lit with pain and I sense without her saying it, that she never forgave her father. Not to his face. Not while he was alive. Knowing my aunt (because I know myself and I am like her) she probably also never forgave herself for what she said. And she probably never spoke her love, even when it pushed to the surface, even forty years later when it was *he* who lay helpless, attached to an oxygen tank. I decide at this moment that when lunch is over I will call my father, wake him from his nap if necessary, and say the words.

The waiter brings the change and lays it at my aunt's elbow. We stand to leave, then suddenly she sits down again and, as if she doesn't want our time together to end on a minor key, here comes a last remembrance, too small and ragged to be called a story. "One year at the beginning of the war five of us came home for Christmas." (That would be five of my grandparents' nine grown children, accompanied by their spouses and families. By then, both of my aunt's children would have arrived safely on this earth.) "The day before Christmas, Dad butchered a hog." She says this as if it were a miracle, something accomplished at great sacrifice and indeed, for those lean times, it was. "He gave us each a tub of lard and some pork. A real treat. We lived on it for months." She begins to laugh and cry at the same time and her brother my father and my grandfather her father, the one she loved but never until this moment forgave, both sit down at the table with us. It is then I know that long after my aunt is dead, I will carry her inside me. Like a snowball that starts small at the top of a hill and barrels down, I will collect these memories, and when I am her age and rolling towards death, I will roll faster, heavier with her stories, carrying the weight of all she has known, and perhaps if I am lucky, the joy.

WHAT IS NOT OURS

I am the hybrid daughter of a farmer and a pilot. My mother's eyes are the rich brown of earth, but my eyes are my father's, the color of skies and distances. When I was ten he took me up for the first time. I remember how clean everything looked, how perfectly planned and ordered. The clouds--whole herds of them!--whiter and fluffier than the dusty sheep whose black faces followed me across the fields of my grandparents' farm. From that day on, my favorite perch was the haymow window where I could watch the world spin on without me. Below in the fading light, my sisters and brothers were living their real, necessary lives--patting together mud pies, combing burdocks from the horses' manes, building the Kon Tiki raft for tomorrow's float down the creek. I liked the view, the tops of heads. From a distance even the cowpies were beautiful, crusted with moonlight. Was this one writer's beginnings? Did the distance, the chosen solitude of that window, frame the world of my first story?

One day many years later, a salesman knocked at the farmhouse door. My grandfather had just huffed in from the pasture where he'd been repairing a fence the lively bull had once again kicked down; manure was dried on his boots. My grandmother was at the sink examining a basket of eggs, still warm and caked with feathers. The salesman, dressed in a navy blue suit, held out a large photograph. It was an aerial view of what appeared to be a perfect toy farm--the gabled house and twin barns looped by a continuous white fence, the fields dotted with tiny horses and cows that stayed obediently where they were planted. An outhouse was tastefully camouflaged in golden foliage. In fact, the whole scene was awash in autumn colors so brilliant they seemed to have been painted on. "It's beautiful," my grandfather sighed. "Whose is it?" Then suddenly, as if he'd just been granted new eyes, he blinked, collapsing happily into the nearest chair. "I never knew it looked like that. Sylvie," he said, turning to my grandmother, "we've got us a beautiful farm."

He bought the photograph, of course, and now, twenty-five

years later, it hangs in my parents' den. I have a photograph of the photograph: twice removed. My copy is slightly blurred around the edges, like a movie frame about to dissolve into flashback. No, it is not the squawking reality of the henhouse, nor the chigger-ridden grasses, nor the slice of rhubarb pie warm from the oven. But I forgive my grandfather for loving the photograph, in that instant, more than he loved the real farm. At times, we all require a proper distance from what is ours, in order to be reminded of its beauty. In her essay "A Sleeve of Rain," Harriett Doerr asks, "As long as I continue to inhabit it, how am I to see it plain and clear?" When I need to fall in love with my life again, I step out of our house, walk to the sidewalk beyond our gate, and peek through our front window. There is the gentle, brown-haired man I first met eighteen years ago. There is my spotted cat Rabbit. There is the picture my aunt painted after her husband died. There is my chair, the afghan still mussed from my recent departure.

The fact that I am able to be simultaneously *in* my own life and *outside* of it is a cause of concern to me. Others assure me this is a normal state for a writer--a necessary state, in fact, for the creation of art. But what price do we pay for this distance? My friend, the photographer, says he has looked through a camera lens so long, he now sees everything that way. "It's hard to enter my own life," he says. "Hard to feel that it is real." Lately I've been thinking of the writer as watcher, and the danger in that. Sometimes I feel like a vulture circling my own life and the lives of others, waiting for the small deaths that will feed me. "Use my life," my mother says, laughing. "Make something of it." I laugh back at her: "Live a life for me. Then I'll write yours." Are writers really cowards, distanced from the stuff of life?

I often say, and I believe it is true, that I want my writing to give something back to the world. Then it occurs to me: Are there not better ways to repay my debt? Teaching throws me into the messy bustle, but occasional fellowship money buys me time to live another way, and I understand why people become hermits. What is the role of the writer in society? If it is true, as Auden said, that poetry makes nothing happen, how can I justify spending my days revising a villanelle while six blocks from my house hungry children sleep in an abandoned bus depot? What is mine, and what is not? These questions wake me each morning; they enter my dreams at night. Yet after years of searching, I am no nearer an answer than I was as a child staring out the haymow window. If anything, the questions have become more complicated and disturbing. The following piece--a mixture of fiction, memoir, journalism, and meditation--is an attempt to worry the question even more, in hopes of moving toward an answer. Although many of the events are not factual, in my mind all of them are true.

*****

Years ago, on a steamy August evening, a dog died on my neighbor's lawn. At first I thought it was a shadow, but as I looked closer I saw the body spread beneath an oak. I called my neighbor. "It's not ours," she said. "I don't know where it came from." No one seemed to know. My neighbor called her husband who called the animal control squad who said they would come as soon as possible.

The next day the dog was stiff, its paws pointing toward the sky. By the third day it was bloated like a dirigible, swollen with summer heat. I remembered a childhood doll, a slick rubber doll stuffed so tight that her arms stuck straight out and the knees would not bend. She had been a gift from Aunt Bessie, a tough, scrawny, childless old woman who lived with our family and with whom I was forced to share a room. I felt obligated to love the doll, but although I tried, I could not bear to touch her, and I never gave her a name.

I watched from the window the progress of death and called my neighbor again. "If it bothers you so much," she said, "bury it yourself." That night I dreamed about the dog. His body hovered over my bed and summoned demons I thought I had buried years ago. I thought of the stories an uncle used to tell about his job during the Depression--raking bodies from rivers. Sometimes, he said, the bodies had swollen three times normal size, and except for the way they floated (face up/face down) you could not distinguish a man from a woman. Some were so distorted you could barely tell they were human.

Weeks after the animal control squad shoveled the carcass into the city truck and carted it away, I began to dream about my students, especially a little girl who one morning had been caged by the principal in the health room because she had bitten the bus driver. And being a writer trained to respect the world of dreams, I considered that the dog may have died on my street for a reason. Maybe I didn't belong here, in this neighborhood of manicured lawns where a dead dog could rot without anyone claiming him. Or worse, maybe I *did* belong here. After all, I had watched it all from my window.

The next year my husband and I bought a brick townhouse in a revitalized inner city neighborhood. Our home is surrounded by restored Victorians and government-owned apartments, blocks from the Salvation Army Women's Shelter, a retirement complex, the school for homeless children, and a century-old cemetery where bearded men lounge across gravestones, drinking from bottles shrouded in paper bags.

The previous owners had equipped the townhouse with an elaborate security system which I was hesitant to use; it seemed more trouble than it was worth. Even when disarmed, the alarm beeped three times whenever a door was opened. To remind us that the system was there if we decided to use it. To remind us of what we'd bought into, a nice home in a high-risk neighborhood.

I moved my writing desk to the front window and each evening I watched the parade: an elderly woman pushing a walker, a tall black woman in an African headdress, and a middle-aged balding man wearing an ascot and holding a cigarette cabaret-style, between thumb and pointer finger. When I looked up again, an old man in greasy slacks was stumbling past my window, stooped beneath the load of a huge garbage bag. I scribbled a few lines in my journal: "A man walks by my window/carrying his life on his back," and

"Even the lightest pack grows heavy/If it's carried long enough."

The boxes were still unpacked, and we'd been in the townhouse only a week when an article in the local section of the newspaper caught my attention. A woman's body had been found less than three blocks away, near a dumpster at the dry cleaners parking lot, next door to a motel fenced with concertina wire. She had been stabbed dozens of times. From where I sat, one level above the street, I could see the dumpster. And like those curious rubberneckers I had always hated, I could not stop looking. For days I found myself studying the dumpster, as if there were something to see. But of course the body was gone, the evidence zip-locked into plastic bags. The neighborhood rumors began--that the dead woman had been a drug addict, a prostitute who had met up with the wrong john. Each morning I searched the paper for news of the investigation. Did the police have a suspect? When would the trial begin? Maybe no one realized she was gone. She had a name, Roberta Francesco, but perhaps she belonged to no one.

Spring came. Some of the street people continued to wear heavy clothing, unwilling to relinquish the protective layers it had taken months to accumulate. But most of them began to molt, slipping out of their winter skins. Each evening on my walk, I stepped over coats, scarves and hats--once a pair of women's shoes, scuffed and worn down at the heels. I thought of Aunt Bessie's advice: "Travel light. Take only what you can't live without." One morning as I emptied trash into the cans at the edge of the yard, I found one can already full: soiled diapers, a milk carton, two high school English books, a hair ribbon, and a pair of blush-tone panty hose, the same shade I wear.

A wrought iron fence surrounds our townhouse, staking our claim all the way to the sidewalk. Inside the fence is a yard too small for grass, but large enough for flowers and plants and three leafy trees. That first spring I planted azaleas and impatiens, varnished an ornate bench, and placed a cherub statue beneath the paper birch. I was amazed at the profusion of squirrels, more than I'd ever seen in our suburban yard. I watched from a distance, admiring their quickness, the fluff and banter of tail, and the way they circle the bark of a tree as if unwrapping a gift. I thought of the shy, curly-lashed squirrels on children's birthday cards, or the tiny helpers in *Bambi* and *Cinderella*, lisping endearments from the movie screen.

The number and variety of birds also amazed me. I placed birdbaths and feeders all over the yard--suet feeders nailed to the oak trunk, a hanging feeder with a plexiglass dome, and a small transparent feeder attached with suction cups to my writing desk window. Within weeks a robin made her nest in the paper birch. And one morning while I was finishing a new poem, the first purple finch arrived and perched on the feeder, inches from my face.

Suddenly I was startled by a thud and rattle coming from upstairs. At first I was frightened; then I remembered that the doors were locked, the alarm set. The rattling continued. I went upstairs and saw a squirrel swinging like a trapeze artist from the chain of the domed feeder, tipping loose seed onto the ground. I clapped my hands and shouted, but the squirrel did not budge. Finally I turned off the alarm system and stepped outside, flailing my arms and shouting until I shooed it away.

This went on all day. Each time I heard the squirrel, I would jump from my desk and run outside to play scarecrow again. Finally I gave up, took the feeder down, and called the hardware store to complain. The manager couldn't believe it. "The Droll Yankee feeder is *guaranteed*," he said. Then, with a hint of admiration in his voice: "Must be *some* squirrel. Try greasing the dome."

A few evenings later I was walking home from the library, where I'd checked out a book on squirrels. When I opened the gate to the courtyard, there was a rustling in the bushes. Over my head the empty feeder was swinging. "Shooo!" I shouted, waving my arms. Then I heard a cry, and a flash of red appeared from the bushes behind the gate. I jumped. It was a blond girl, not more than fifteen, holding a baby and a diaper bag. Her eyes were wild with fear. "I had to change him," she said. "There's nowhere else." After I calmed myself, I spoke. "It's okay, don't worry. But what about the shelter?" We were barely a foot apart, separated only by the bars of the iron fence. She shook her head. "He's waiting for me on the steps. I saw him." The baby began to cry and she stuck a pacifier into his mouth, then turned quickly and hurried away, heading in the opposite direction from the shelter.

The book is open before me. Squirrel. From the Greek, *Skiouros*. Shadow-tail. I am thinking about the dead dog and remembering scraps from a poem that never found its completion. Doppelganger: the double-goer, flip side of ourselves. And months before, a poem about the placenta, how ancient Egyptians worshipped it and saved it to bury years later with the body, fearful that if it were loose, it would roam the world, searching for its other half. In one draft I'd called the placenta a dark sister. Shadow-tail: what tails us when our back is turned. Twenty years ago, alone and out of a job and too proud to ask for money from my parents, I stood in line for food stamps. What I remember most is what the government worker did *not* say, how silently and methodically he counted out the coupons, without once meeting my gaze. I was invisible to him--and *nothing*, I realized at that moment, could be worse than that. Not even the hard eyes of the grocery clerk, a yellowed woman who audibly sneered when I handed her the coupons.

My mother once came to her own front door, in the midst of a family reunion, and I would not let her in. This was only one of many pranks and disguises she managed successfully throughout the years, but it is the one I remember most clearly, perhaps because I recall it with sadness. She had slipped out the back door while no one was looking and, in the flurry of activity, was not missed. When the doorbell rang, I was coming around the corner from the kitchen, my plate loaded with the pot-luck fare of such occasions. My hands were occupied, so I nodded to my nephew to open the door. An old woman stood a few feet away on the top step of the darkening porch. She was wearing a heavy coat that nearly reached her shoes. Her face was grimy, her gray hair oily and matted, partly concealed by a woolen stocking cap. Large glasses, speckled with grease, sat on the edge of her nose, the lenses so thick that they seemed to send her eyes wandering in different directions. My nephew reached for my arm. The old woman was staring hard at my plate, and I was about to step between her and the open door when she spoke. It was only one word--"Ma'am"--but something in the voice gave her away. She must have seen the change in my eyes, for suddenly my mother laughed, pulled off the glasses, and walked through the door, grabbing a biscuit from my plate.

I was seventeen when I saw my first beggar, although at the time I didn't recognize her as one. My boyfriend had driven me over the border for a day's sightseeing in Tijuana, my first trip out of the States. He had warned me: "Don't stop. Don't make eye contact. They're everywhere." We got out of the car and walked the streets. I was caught up in the moment, the cinematic scope of it-- cardboard shacks, the smell of tortillas, flocks of barefoot children fluttering in the dust. A little girl stepped out of the crowd, a splash of local color. Her eyes and hair were black and she was holding a bouquet of huge crepe paper flowers. She began to tug at my skirt. "Dollar each?"

"Come on," my boyfriend said.

The girl grabbed tighter to my skirt and would not let go. "Dollar each? Dollar each?"

I chose a yellow flower, the biggest brightest one, and gave her three dollars, feeling special that I had been chosen, out of all the other tourists in the crowd. Then I turned a corner into the marketplace and saw, floating above my head, hundreds of identical crepe paper flowers, each bunch attached to the hands of a small brown child who was waving frantically in my direction.

At the neighborhood homeowner's meeting, everyone is cheering the news: an uptown bank has proposed buying the property where the women's shelter sits. By next summer, if everything goes as planned, the shelter will be moved. "It's not the women themselves," the moderator says. "Or the children. But where there are women, there will be men." He is talking about the field across from the shelter. Every morning it is littered with bottles, blankets, used syringes, condoms. Two homes in the neighborhood have been broken into recently and last week an elderly man was mugged in the alley behind my house. I am more careful about walking alone now, and I never open the door to strangers. When my husband is out of town, I keep the portable alert-button beside the bed.

The moderator continues. "The Braggio's house, next door to the shelter, has been on the market for two years. We've got to protect our property values."

I sit quietly, unsure of how to feel. I have always known the poor and homeless exist among us. Some of them are my students. I see the soiled clothes and ill-fitting shoes. I smell the poverty, and am ashamed to say that after twenty years of experience I have developed a method of breathing around some children without actually inhaling their stench. I know which students have lice and which ones I dare not touch without risking infection. Still, I believe that I care. Occasionally I let one boy sleep during class because, as his journal reveals, there has been shooting outside his apartment and he's been awake all night. I help where I can, like the time I reported the cigarette burns on a little girl's hand, but at the end of the school day I have always been able to go home and close myself off until the next morning. I can't do that anymore. Now they're coming to *me*, into my bushes, into the alley beside my house.

The moderator calls for discussion before the informal vote, a show of hands in favor of the buyout. The truth is, I want to protect what is mine. I have worked hard for what I have and I believe I deserve it. Yet when I stand, words float to me, through me, as if someone else were speaking them. "I think we should keep the shelter here," I say. "The problem won't go away. They'll just put it in someone else's neighborhood."

Mr. Braggio turns to face me. "You wouldn't say that if they urinated in *your* yard. If it were *your* house that wouldn't sell." Later that night, it occurs to me that I was able to speak only because I knew my words wouldn't matter. I could count on the others to outvote me.

The next morning I'm at the Women's Shelter. "I want to help," I tell the director.

"Who doesn't?" Her voice is tired. "Can you answer phones?"

This is not what I had in mind. I want to do something important--work with the children, help them write poems, counsel the women, listen to their problems.

"Or scrub the kitchen. Erma can use the help." She can read my eyes--save the dolphins, save the world. "A lady called yesterday," she says. "She wanted to *help*. I asked her, 'Can you type? We need a new rule list.' She said she wanted to do something *important*, to help the women. I said, 'Lady, if one person had all the answers, these women wouldn't be here.'" I look around the dayroom. One woman is weaving invisible tapestries in the air.

"Phones will be fine," I say.

"Have a seat. There are two lines. Do *not* tell callers who's here. If they ask for someone, tell them you'll take a message and *if* that woman happens to be here and *if* she wants to talk to them, she'll get back in touch." The phone rings and I reach to answer it. She places her hand over mine. "Don't forget. Some of these women are running for their lives."

Summer stretches itself long and lazy. On the benches the men grab their sleeping spaces for the night. I wish I could see inside each one, to know who is a Vietnam vet down on his luck, who is a father searching for a job so he can reunite with the wife and son staying at the shelter, who is a thief, who has hurt women like me before, who could have been my grandfather ten years ago when his mind suddenly took off and left him alone, babbling. I want to speak a simple "Hello" to these men, to return what is probably a harmless nod. But I am afraid. Last week I jogged two blocks too far, near the dumpster where the murdered woman had been found. A young man in filthy clothes shot me a frightening glance. I sped up and crossed the street, but not before he had unzipped his pants, calling out, "How 'bout a piece of this, bitch? A big piece of this?"

There are twelve of us in the circle. Twelve women of all ages, races, and sizes. Our instructor is a large, beautiful black man named Tobias, an ex-Marine with a shaved head, a black belt in Karate, and what Aunt Bessie would call "killer eyes." But his laugh is easy and warm. I like him. He either likes me a lot or he hates me, I can't tell which, because when he learns my father was a Marine, he singles me out. "Front and center, McClanahan," he shouts drill-sergeant style. "Higher on that kick. Put it there, McClanahan. Right into the knee." His face is masked to protect his eyes, and he is padded from shoulders to shins. "You can't hurt me. Kick!" And when I'm too slow, "You'd be dead by now," as he spins away and grabs me from behind.

"If the thought of putting someone's eye out makes you sick," he tells us the next week, "get out now. This isn't basketweaving. This is life and death. You've got to become an animal, get down to his level. Out-animal him. McClanahan, front and center."

By the third week, seven women have dropped out. The remaining five have grown claws and fur. The louder Tobias yells, the quicker our kicks, our punches. We work with partners, one on one, alternating being the attacker and the attackee. ("No one is a victim," Tobias says. "You have to consent to be a victim.") "Forget the groin. If I'm high on dope, I won't feel it. Go for the eyes. The eyes and the knees. Scream. Bite. Women always forget their teeth. Bite and run. Kick, scream, and run. Remain cool, but do whatever it takes. Out-animal him."

The final exam is five minutes one-on-one against Tobias. We can call time by raising our left hand. If we do that, there will be no certificate, but we can retake the exam as many times as we like. I go early to class, lift weights, practice my kicks in the mirror. Five minutes is not so long, I think. I can do it.

He calls me first, of course, and I leap in, cocky, firing on all pistons. "Pace yourself," he says through the mask. He grabs me around the neck. I lower my chin and simulate a bite on his wrist. He drops his hands. "One minute," the assistant shouts. I am panting. Blood is thumping in my head. I position my three middle fingers and go for what should be his eyes, but miss. My hands slide off his slick head. I thrust out my right leg, aiming for his kneecap. I lose my balance and fall, but have been trained to keep rolling, so I roll away from him, to the edge of the mat, then I'm up, and he's coming at me. We circle awhile, and when he leaps for me, I dart in the opposite direction. My chest is burning. "Three minutes," the assistant calls. Years of jogging, aerobics, pool laps, have not prepared me for this. I grab my chest, thinking I will die if I keep going. I start to lift my arm, no certificate for me this time. But Tobias refuses to let me fail. He grabs my arm and rolls me over until my face is pressed against the mat. He is panting. His breath is hot on my neck as he leans down and hisses, "Well, McClanahan. Your life or mine?" "Four minutes," says the assistant. I lie flat against the mat, the blood thrumming in my head. I have never been so hot. I am sure I am dying. Then something clicks in. I clench my teeth and scream into the mat and, simultaneously, slide one arm out from under me, searching blindly for the inside of his leg, right above the kneecap. I grab a knot of flesh and pinch, pinch, until he squeezes out a "Good move" and rolls off me. "Time," yells the assistant. I stagger to my knees, then to my feet. The four other women are clapping. My heart is beating behind my eyes. I have bitten my tongue, and blood drips down my shirt.

I am at my desk watching a purple finch at the feeder

attached to the window. It is the only feeder left. Last week I finally gave up, even on the Droll Yankee guaranteed against squirrels. For days I had endured the rat-gray fur, the clack of claws on the feeding tray and even the attacks on the suet cage nailed to a tree. Nothing I did seemed to matter--not greasing the dome, not shouting, not my hands let loose like weapons.

I go upstairs to pour more coffee, and when I return I notice that the feeder is on the ground. Sunflower seeds are scattered around it. The window is scratched, and there are two dusty circles where the suction cups had gripped. A bird would be too light to dislodge the feeder, yet I see no way a squirrel could get to it. I walk outside and replace the feeder, fill it with seed, come back inside, and settle at my desk to watch. After only a few minutes, I hear it--a clicking, a scraping. A brown head appears at the bottom of the window; then the body, scrambling upwards, one side clawing the wooden frame, the other scratching the glass. Now the squirrel is halfway up the window, propelled by I know not what. A leap, and it is on the top of the feeder. It stands upright, on hind legs, and spreads itself against the glass, directly in front of my eyes. I have never been this close--never seen the white underbelly and, count them, six rubbery teats. Never seen the whiskers twitching, the slick black eyes, and how, with a perfect five-fingered hand, she stuffs into the pocketbook of her jaw the seed which will feed her babies.

It's Friday evening at the shelter and the phones are ringing off the hook, the men calling their women. "It's always like this on Friday," clucks Erma the cook. "Yessir. Friday. Forgiveness fills the air. Plus it's payday," she adds. I take messages from the callers and post them on the bulletin board, where a group of women are gathered. Some tear up the messages, a few tuck them into their pockets, but most line up at the phone. First in line is the young blond woman, balancing the baby on her hip.

Across the room, the Tapestry-Weaver is conducting a symphony in the air. I wish we could all hear it; she is the only one smiling. Beside her is the Plant Lady, as Erma calls her. Each evening when the Plant Lady comes in from the streets, her arms are loaded with branches and flowers she has collected from neighborhood yards like mine. She holds them in her lap during dinner and when it is time to go to bed, she arranges them carefully on her cot the way I imagine a mother bird plumps up her nest.

When all the women have made their phone calls, I turn to the other line of women waiting to get a bed for the night. My job is to check their names against the rolodex where we keep the records and I.D. snapshots of anyone who has ever stayed at the shelter. "Last name?" I ask the dark thin woman. "Francesco," she answers, and the name jars my memory. I flip through the file and do not find this woman's card. But, yes, there is the other one, the card for the dead woman. Roberta Francesco: the signature is striking in its childlike simplicity, each letter perfectly rounded and distinct. But the face is blurred, as if the woman had turned away at the last second, just as the photographer snapped the picture. She might be anyone.

My husband is out of town, so Erma drives me the three blocks home and waits until I get inside and flick the lights twice--my signal that everything is okay. A woman alone develops systems to assure her safety. On nights when I leave late from a friend's house, I call to let her know I've gotten home all right. We check on each other; otherwise, how will anyone know if something goes wrong? Last week the paper reported that a widow in Italy was dead for days before anyone called the authorities. To make matters worse, she had died in plain view of her neighbors, sitting in a rocking chair on her balcony, a blanket wrapped around her legs. She sat there three days and three nights before anyone became suspicious. Aunt Bessie died alone too, between hospital shifts. My mother had gone to the cafeteria for another cup of coffee, and the night nurse was a few minutes late starting her rounds.

I set the alarm, get into my pajamas, and settle back on the couch to watch an old Cary Grant movie. It's noisy outside. Fridays are always noisy--the fire engines, teenagers with their radios blasting, the late-night crowd from the neighborhood pub. But by the time the movie is over, the street noise has calmed. I get into bed, but I can't sleep. I keep seeing the dead woman's face, blurry yet somehow unforgettable. Downstairs the icemaker purrs, clanks into a new cycle. I get up to check the doors and windows and to place the alert-button beside my bed. Finally I climb back under the covers and, after much tossing, drop heavily into a dream.

I'm trying to open the front door, but it won't budge. I lean on the door and push slowly with all my strength. There, on the porch, are dozens of dead dogs, face-up on the concrete. Flies and maggots have already begun their work. There is nowhere to step, nowhere to place my feet where there is not a dog, stiffening as I watch.

At first I think the voices are part of my dream, but they keep on long after my eyes are open. My mouth feels fuzzy and the sheets are sticky. I hear the voices again. Pub-goers, I think, and turn my pillow to its cooler side. The voices get louder and more distinct, splitting into two voices, a man's and a woman's. They seem to be arguing. But that's not unusual on a Friday night. They're probably walking home, they've had too much to drink, it happens all the time.

Then the woman screams, a long urgent scream, and my heart starts to gallop as if *I'm* being pursued. I lie trembling, and when she screams again, I leap out of bed and down the steps to the landing. The outside light illuminates the porch. Beyond the gate, it is too dark to make out shapes, but when the scream comes again, I trace it to the alley behind my house. I should go outside and yell, I should help her, two against one, but what if he has a knife or a gun, what if he runs away and comes back for me another night. I stand motionless with my hand on the doorknob. By the time I get to the phone to dial 911, a patrol car is at the curb. Someone has already reported it. How long did I wait, where did I go during those moments, what was I thinking? I am too ashamed to go outside where my neighbors are gathering.

The patrolman is helping the woman to the car. It is the young blond mother. One of her shoes is missing and she is limping, leaning onto his arm. Another patrol car arrives.

Two officers jump out and run into the alley, their flashlights bouncing, sending arcs of light into my yard--across the cherub statue, the birdbath and the garden bench, flickering through the leaves of the paper birch and the bars of the iron fence.

The bulldozers came last week. It did not take long. Now there is nothing but rubble and dust and a huge wound in the earth where the shelter once sat. Even the foundation is gone, as if ripped out by its very roots. I have not seen the new facility two miles away, but I've heard that it's larger, more modern, closer to the other county services the inhabitants require. The women who once lived in the shelter are gone too, except for The Plant Lady. From my writing desk window I watch her each morning as she strolls through the neighborhood, gathering all the greenery she can carry.

I walk past Mr. Braggio's house where the sign in the front yard reads "Under Contract." The park across the street is clean of debris, and two of my neighbor's children are climbing the bars of the jungle gym. It seems odd to see children I know; I had grown accustomed to the shelter children. I cross the street and walk past the fountain and down the shaded path where The Plant Lady sits on a bench beneath the oak. I wave at her, but she does not wave back. In her lap are several green branches and a newspaper which she is tearing into pieces. Her gestures are quick and nervous as a squirrel's, and there is anger in her eyes. Her breath is coming in hard pants. She rips at the newspaper violently as if to destroy each word. When she hears me, she looks up, but only for a minute, then she is back at her task. Something in her eyes tells me not to speak, so I keep on walking until I get to a large shrub. From behind the leafy camouflage, I can observe her without revealing myself. Yesterday's headlines float around her; stories too, all those lines some writer spent himself on. Then as I watch, she begins gathering all the tiny pieces, the broken words, fluffing them into a pillow she will rest her head on tonight.

WORKS CITED

Auden, W. H., "In Memory of W. B. Yeats," *Collected Poems*, New York: Random House, 1945.

Doerr, Harriet, "A Sleeve of Rain," *The Writer on Her Work, Vol. II*. Ed. by Janet Sternburg, New York: W. W. Norton & Co., 1992.